SARASOTA'S
ASOLO

a
HISTORY
of the
STATE
THEATRE
of
FLORIDA

Brad Wallace

THE History PRESS

Published by The History Press
Charleston, SC 29403
www.historypress.net

Front cover, bottom, left to right: *Guys and Dolls*; Burton Clarke and Robert Strane in *King Lear*, *photo by Gary Sweetman*; SaRa Schabach in *Mirandolina*, *photo by Frank Atura*.
Back cover, top right: Barbara Reid, Isa Thomas and Walter Rhodes in *Little Mary Sunshine*.
All images courtesy of the Asolo Theatre unless otherwise noted.

First published 2011

Manufactured in the United States

ISBN 978.1.60949.120.8

Library of Congress Cataloging-in-Publication Data
Wallace, Brad.
Sarasota's Asolo : a history of the state theatre of Florida / Brad Wallace.
p. cm.
Includes bibliographical references.
ISBN 978-1-60949-120-8
1. Asolo Theater (Sarasota, Fla.)--History. 2. Theaters--Florida--Sarasota--History--20th century. 3. Theater and society--Florida--Sarasota. I. Title.
PN2277.S43W35 2011
792.5'09777--dc22
2010052601

Dedicated to Richard G. Fallon

Contents

Preface

Asolo, often called the city of a hundred horizons, is first mentioned by Pliny the Elder in the first century A.D. as a flourishing Roman colony. A temple of Diana, an aqueduct, baths and a theater were already built, as well as some sort of fortification on the outcropping of rock above the center of the town, where the castello now stands.
—The Asolo Theater and the John and Mabel Ringling Museum of Art, *a booklet published by the Ringling Museum in 1952*

There was a Texas lady named Margo Jones who loved the theatre so much that she became obsessed with the idea of creating a national theatre that would make first-class professional productions available to people across the country. Her dream was to establish twenty theatres in major metropolitan areas that would produce both the classics and the original works of young, struggling playwrights. That was in the 1940s.

Today, there are more than seventy members of the League of Resident Theatres (LORT) representing regions both large and small. They can be found in Oregon and Alabama, in California and Virginia, in Utah and New York and in Florida, where, because of Margo Jones's passion and leadership, I have had a home base to work as an actor for more than fifty years.

The history of each of these regional theatres is, no doubt, unique. But the Asolo's history is, in one respect, "more unique" than the rest. Other regional theatres have grown from the example of Margo Jones, who inspired individuals to build companies and, in time, structures where those companies could perform. The Asolo Theatre Festival, on the other hand, was the product of a structure that already existed.

Preface

Asolo, Italy, is about an hour's drive north of Venice. The Asolo Theatre was originally constructed there in the audience hall of a fifteenth-century castle and completed in 1798. In 1933, this beautiful Baroque theatre was carefully dismantled, crated and sold to an antique dealer in Venice—not the entire building, of course, but the exquisite parts decorating the horseshoe-shaped interior, which was so common to theatres built during that period.

The Asolo was purchased by the State of Florida in 1950 and, in 1957, was reconstructed in a new wing on the grounds of the Ringling Museum of Art in Sarasota, Florida. In 1960, a group of young actors produced a summer festival of Restoration and eighteenth-century plays in the theatre. And there begins a story that, to my mind, has been guided by the hands of Providence.

Henry Hewes of the *Saturday Review of Literature* wrote, "There are two theaters in North America where one feels it is worth the price of admission simply to enter and be seated. One is the Stratford, Ontario Festival Theatre, and the other is the Asolo Theatre in Sarasota, Florida." For the same magazine, James Thrall Soby opined of the Asolo, "The theater, complete to an astonishing degree, is not only one of the most important architectural documents ever brought to this country, but a thoroughly rewarding work of art in its own right."

During its early years in Italy, the theatre attracted some of Europe's greatest talents as both performers and audience members. When Katharine Cornell, the distinguished actress, visited the Asolo Theatre in Sarasota in the late 1950s, she recalled the inspiration of the great Italian actress Eleonora Duse: "Standing in the theatre where Duse had played in her own youth, we felt the continuing life of a tradition. This is perhaps the best reason for taking care of older works of art in museums: The talent and imagination that humanity has been able to show earlier can continue to be the stimulus for the best that we can try to be."

For those who have supported the Asolo for some time, I imagine this history will be a walk down memory lane. For the newcomer, it may be a book of revelations, or perhaps a small look at the potential, both good and bad, which lies behind any artistic business. But my main purpose in writing about the Asolo is to highlight the lessons that I believe are there. In doing so, I have tried to editorialize as little as possible, hoping that my story is adequately told and does not need excessive comment; that an objective presentation of events will better highlight what has been harmful and what has been constructive during the life of this very successful regional theatre.

Acknowledgements

I would like to thank the many friends who spent time being interviewed and talking with me about the facts and figures that were essential to the composition of this history. I would like to thank the many local journalists, especially Charlie Husking, who recorded a blow-by-blow account of how the Asolo has evolved over the years. I am indebted to the photographers, especially Gary Sweetman (www.garysweetman.com), for generously contributing so many of the photographs that were used. I owe a great deal to my long-suffering wife, Marian, who supported me during the years of research and writing and who contributed her own ideas as to what has happened. And finally, I have special thanks for my daughter, Hannah, who edited the book and gleefully corrected her father's mistakes.

Chapter 1

A Providential Friendship

In 1946, by placing the Ringling property under the jurisdiction of the State Board of Control, which exercises supervision over all Florida institutions of higher learning, those in authority made it clear that they considered the Sarasota institution much more than a fabulous tourist attraction—that they wished and intended it to become a vital force of education.

—Sarasota Herald-Tribune, *April 8, 1951*

The Florida State Board of Control assumed responsibility for Sarasota's Ringling Museum of Art in 1946 and shortly thereafter appointed the museum's first director, A. Everette "Chick" Austin. Thus began a series of events that would grow into one of Florida's most important cultural institutions.

The seeds had been planted years earlier.

Through the 1920s and '30s, Chick Austin had earned a national reputation as director of the Wadsworth Athenaeum in Hartford, Connecticut, America's oldest public art museum. A lover of all the arts, Austin's passion for theatre was especially pronounced. Even after establishing himself as the nation's preeminent museum director (as decreed by Paul J. Sachs, then director of Harvard's Fogg Museum), Austin created his own summer theatre in New Hampshire—purchasing the necessary equipment himself and then participating in productions as an actor and director.

Among Austin's close friends and business associates was Adolph Loewi, an antique dealer and the German consul to Venice, Italy. It was Loewi who introduced Austin to the jewel-box theatre that had stood in the city of Asolo, Italy, since 1798.

Asolo, Italy, today.

"I often went up to the hill town of Asolo from Venice on buying trips in the 1920s and '30s," Loewi recalled in an interview years later with the *Sarasota Herald-Tribune*. "I had seen and admired the theatre." That theatre remained intact in its original setting, Queen Catherine Cornaro's fifteenth-century *castello* in Asolo, until 1933, when it was discovered by Mussolini.

For a year or two, Loewi feared the worst. In the mid-1930s, during lunch with Asolo resident and composer Gian Francesco Malipiera, Loewi learned that Mussolini's fascist government regarded the theatre as decadent and thought that it did not "meet the exigencies of the day," said Malipiera. Mussolini decreed that all the theatre's rococo decorations should be removed from the *castello*.

One might expect that Mussolini's government would have then destroyed the offending parts. Instead, for reasons that may never be known, the theatre's decorative pieces were carefully removed, crated and placed in an old warehouse. Once he learned of its location, Loewi almost immediately offered to buy the parts. The mayor of Asolo happily complied, saying, "It's no good to us lying there taking up space."

Loewi shipped the theatre to a large warehouse in Venice, Italy, where there was room to assemble the proscenium and the tiers of boxes. "That is where Chick Austin saw it for the first time in 1937 or 1938," he later recalled, "and fell in love with it."

At the outset of World War II, Loewi moved to Los Angeles, California, and started a new business. Then, in 1946, Austin was appointed director of the Ringling Museum. "The very next day," Loewi recalled, "Chick phoned me. 'Adolph,' he said, 'now is the time for the theatre! It will be a perfect addition to the museum!'"

Austin's decisiveness allowed him to outmaneuver a number of other potential American buyers. Among them, the well-known film actor, Vincent Price, had wanted to build a home for the Asolo in California, but he didn't move fast enough.

After some lobbying by Austin, the Florida State Board of Control purchased the theatre in early 1950 for $8,000, which included shipping costs. It arrived in Florida, said Loewi, "in a packing case the size of a freight-car" in the summer of 1950.

While Austin worked to establish the theatre's edifice in its new Sarasota quarters, the artistic company that would call the Asolo home had also begun to take shape.

In the spring of 1948, two years before the theatre arrived in this country, Florida State University art professor Adolph Karl suggested collaborating with the Ringling Museum to sponsor a celebration of the arts in Sarasota. Austin, an enthusiastic supporter of arts education, embraced this idea. The collaboration included a year-round educational program for children, as well as an annual arts seminar to be held on the museum grounds.

Austin felt that studying all fine arts media, and the mutual influence each had on the others, was the proper way to approach aesthetics. In a biography (*Magician of the Modern*) Eugene R. Gaddis quotes Austin saying, "The function of a museum is more than merely showing pictures. The museum is the place to integrate the arts and bring them to life."

In April 1948, the first Sarasota Arts Seminar began a successful three-week run. (Austin gave the majority of lectures.) Beatrice B. Williams, head of the FSU art department, and Karl A. Bickel of the State Board of Control made the welcoming statements. "This seminar," said Williams, "is the first of an annual series, and represents a new departure for both the university and the museum. It is off to a flying start." The State Board of Control expressed its approval in a statement: "The board is greatly pleased with the progress shown in the rehabilitation of the Ringling Museum under the energetic management and direction of Mr. Austin."

Over the years, and thanks to Austin's reputation as a premier museum director, the seminar would attract an impressive assemblage of lecturers who hailed from the likes of the Metropolitan Museum of Art, the National Gallery of Art and the Museum of Modern Art, as well as Columbia, Harvard, Yale, the American Ballet and more. True to Austin's belief in the interaction of the arts, the seminar's speakers lectured on painting, sculpture, architecture, music, dance and film.[1]

But theatrical performances were not integrated into the seminar's program until two years later, when FSU was invited to perform a play for the closing night, April 15, 1950. For the initial production, FSU's Dr. George McCalmon directed Moliere's *The School for Husbands*. The play was rehearsed in Tallahassee and brought to Sarasota on a school bus driven by Charles I. Reimer, who had joined the FSU faculty in 1947 as technical director and designer for the speech department's theatre area. In a taped interview in 1976, Charlie vividly recalled the particulars of the trip he took in the spring of 1950:

> *We traveled on a school bus that had had some seats removed for the lighting and costumes. We left early Friday morning, around five or six o'clock, got to St. Petersburg around noon, lunched there and then drove directly to the Ringling Museum. Our stage was the steps on the south side of the courtyard (the audience would sit on the grass), and after the scenery was set up we'd have a rehearsal in the afternoon, and maybe a speed run the next morning.*

This marked the first time that FSU student actors performed at the Ringling Museum. The event was so popular that each seminar through 1959 ended with an FSU production.

In a fitting token to John Ringling's Sarasota legacy, that first production borrowed extra lighting from the circus.

After the success of *The School for Husbands*, supporters hoped the museum could add a special wing to house Austin's little theatre from Asolo. But for various reasons (including, perhaps, the expense of the Korean War), public funds were not available. Instead, Austin made plans to temporarily install the Asolo Theatre in gallery 21, at the southeast corner of the museum. The installation included a usable stage, but structural problems and a lack of space prevented the upper two tiers of the theatre's boxes from being used, thus limiting the seating capacity to fewer than two hundred.

---

1. Lecturers included A. Hyatt Mayor, curator of prints at the Metropolitan Museum of Art; Rudolph Wittkower of Columbia University; Dr. John Coolidge, who succeeded Sachs as director of Harvard's Fogg Museum; Iris Barry, curator of the film library of the Museum of Modern Art; Ralph Twitchell, a nationally known Sarasota architect; George Evans, docent of the National Gallery of Art, Washington, D.C.; Josef Albers, chairman of the department of design at Yale University; Lincoln Kirstein, director general of the American Ballet; and Andrew C. Ritchie, director of painting and sculpture at the Museum of Modern Art.

The first Florida State University student production at the Ringling Museum (Moliere's *The School for Husbands*), 1950. *Photo by Charles Reimer.*

Still, with the decorative parts of the theatre in place, two eighteenth-century chamber operas (Mozart's *Bastien et Bastienne* and Pergolesi's *La Serva Padrona*) opened the new performance space on February 26, 1952. Austin designed the set and costumes for the Mozart, and distinguished designer Eugene Berman designed the Pergolesi. Singers from the New York City Opera performed, and the musicians had been assembled from New York, Sarasota and Bradenton. The museum was decorated in an Italian motif for the opening, and the audience arrived in black tie. "The weather was gracious to the occasion," wrote Betty Burket for Sarasota's *The News*. "Under a full moon shining down on the gardens, the audience, in formal evening array, graced the corridors and courtyard at intermission."

The first FSU production in gallery 21, *La Parisienne* by Henry Becque, closed the seminar that April 1952. It was the third production the college had brought to the museum, and because the popularity of the plays was increasing substantially, tickets in the future were available only to those who registered for the lectures.

Two years later, on the final evening of the 1954 seminar (by then relabeled "symposium"), the FSU company performed Karel Capek's *The Insect Comedy*. The cast included Robert Strane (as Felix the butterfly poet) and Eberle Thomas (as Mr. Beetle), then undergraduate students at FSU. This was their first performance in Sarasota; the two men would eventually become major figures in the Asolo's most crucial years of development.

During the fall of 1954, Austin submitted a proposal to the City of Sarasota for a new building. It was accepted. Marion I. Manley, a Palm Beach architect, would design the new structure in collaboration with Guy Fulton, the architect for the State Board of Control. Work began in 1955 and was scheduled to be completed in the fall of 1956. Delays, however, pushed the grand opening back to the spring of 1957.

Sadly, A. Everette Austin died on March 29, 1957, after a long battle with cancer. The man responsible for the acquisition and preservation of the Asolo Theatre did not live to see it restored in the building that would, for the next thirty-two years, be a model for Florida's educational and cultural life.

Years earlier, Barbara Williams's welcoming remarks for the first seminar best described Austin's lifelong passion for crossing artistic barriers for the betterment of all art: "He has considered the basic concepts and problems of the architect, sculptor, painter and designer of the minor arts, and has tied up their problems with those of the non-visual arts (music and literature) and with ballet and opera in which many arts are combined."

Kenneth Donahue, Austin's assistant and the museum's curatorial librarian, was appointed the new director.

The new building allowed the theatre to be widened slightly to make room for two rear entrances. The posts that originally had supported the upper tiers could be removed because the upper floors were now cantilevered. Beyond that, the Asolo was very much as it had been in Italy.

The grand opening for the Asolo's new home was again postponed until early 1958 for "finishing touches"—though it hosted its first performances in April 1957, just one month after Austin's death. On April 27, 1957, the

The historic Asolo interior (1957 to 2004). *Photo by Ted Lagerberg.*

closing evening of the symposium, FSU students presented productions of *Oedipus the King* by Sophocles and *The Man Who Married a Dumb Wife* by Anatole France, which "delighted a capacity audience in the Asolo Theatre," according to a review in the *Sarasota Herald-Tribune.*

Though accounts at the time gave no grand declarations, we can safely assume that these were the first two FSU student productions to be played in the new Asolo wing.

Sarasota's new, permanent Asolo Theatre celebrated its grand opening on Friday evening, January 10, 1958. The New York City Opera Company performed Mozart's *The Abduction From the Seraglio.* Foster Harmon, a much beloved patron of the arts in Sarasota, gave an account: "The Saturday performance was followed by a fabulous ball in the John Ringling residence. The affair was Sarasota's most colorful social event of many seasons and attracted international coverage in *Life* magazine of February 17." Entertainment included fireworks, jugglers and acrobats.

That spring, the 1958 symposium opened with a welcoming address by Dr. Albert B. Martin, vice-president of FSU. J. Russell Tynes Jr., the managing director of *Harper's Magazine*, gave a lecture titled "What is the matter with American taste?" in which he argued for the legitimacy of the Ringling Museum's growing mission: "There is a tremendous spread of interest in the arts. Music is better off than ever on the appreciation side, and while in theater Broadway does badly on the practical end, little theaters all over the country keep up interest. The small museums have become enormously more important in the last 15 years. They pull the various arts, including music and theater, together and are much more used than ever before."

The historic Asolo exterior (1957 to 2004).

Arthur Dorlag.

Charles Reimer.

The closing FSU production on April 26, 1958, was Ben Jonson's *The Alchemist.* The show's enthusiastic response generated terrific demand for the 1959 symposium's final event, Clifford Odet's *The Country Girl*, which played on April 23 and 24. That show featured several people who would become vitally important to the Asolo over the years, including then FSU professor Richard G. Fallon, who directed, and cast members Howard Millman as Bernie Dodd, Eberle Thomas as Frank Elgin and Isa Davidson as Georgie Elgin. Charlie Reimer was the technical director, and the costumes were designed by Bill King.

In the audience for one performance was Dr. Arthur H. Dorlag, a specialist in Restoration and eighteenth-century plays and operas. He had just become head of FSU's theatre department (no longer "area") and he was seeing the Asolo Theatre for the first time.

Art Dorlag quickly envisioned a new annual festival, with the Asolo its perfect setting, featuring Baroque plays and operas. "Shakespearean and modern theatrical festivals dot the countryside every summer," he later wrote, "but nowhere has there been a presentation in repertory of the great theatrical achievements of the 17th and 18th centuries on the continent and of English productions from the death of Shakespeare to the beginning of the 19th century."

Art Dorlag and Charlie Reimer drove back to Tallahassee together. According to Art, it was during that trip that the two laid down the very first plans for a summer festival in the Asolo Theatre.

Chapter 2

The Early Summer Festivals

The question of whether repertory can survive in America is and always has been an economic matter...It's never been a question of whether there's a better way of doing it artistically.

—New York Times, *January 17, 1986*

The creation of a complete theatre festival was, of course, daunting. Although Art Dorlag received enthusiastic support form FSU president Robert Strozier and Ringling Museum director Kenneth Donahue, there was still some concern that the state and the museum would have objections. FSU professor Dick Fallon, who had directed the previous year's *Country Girl* for the Sarasota symposium, met with Art and Charlie Reimer after their noteworthy drive back to Tallahassee. Dick became an enthusiastic supporter of the project, and he visited Governor Leroy Collins to outline the plans:

> *I went to see the governor in Tallahassee and told him what we wanted to do. "The difficulty," I said, "is that the entities are all separate: one is the Board of Regents and the other the Ringling Museum board* [the members of both boards were appointed by the governor]*." The governor said, "I think the best way to handle the situation is for me to write the boards and instruct them to allow a series of plays to be performed in the Asolo Theatre during the summer of 1960."*

If not for the initiative of Dick Fallon and the support of Governor Collins, it's possible that the first summer festival would never have happened.

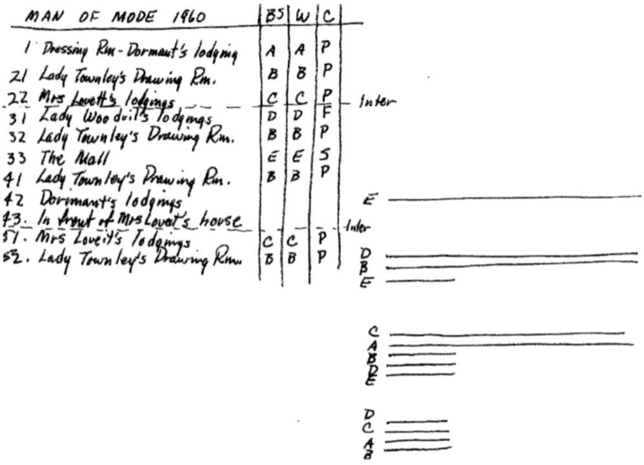

A Charles Reimer ground plan for wing-and-shutter scenery. (The guides on the stage left side are not shown.)

The final scene from the Asolo's 1963 production of Sheridan's *The Rivals*. Note the perspective created by the wing-and-shutter scenery.

In addition to his collaborative talks with Dick and Art Dorlag, Charlie Reimer literally built the foundation for the first summer festival. Charlie began building sets in January 1960. He worked until mid-July, seven days a week and virtually without assistance, to build more than one hundred four- by eight-foot canvas "flats" on which various scenes could be painted, in addition to finding or making props and furniture for all the shows. When considering Art's preferred period—Baroque—the emphasis was on authenticity. The scenery for one of the shows, for example, was a reproduction of the play's original seventeenth-century set.

A wing-and-shutter scenery system, which would have been common in England and on the Continent during the Baroque period, was used for productions. This system employed guides on the stage floor (parallel to the footlights) and corresponding guides flown from above. There were four matching positions stage left and stage right, and each position could hold up to five different flats for five different settings. Four- by eight-foot "wings" (flats) in three downstage positions on either side of the stage, and eight- by eight-foot "shutters" (double flats) that could come together in the two upstage positions, were painted to give a sense of perspective. A company member was assigned to each position and on a signal (usually a pennywhistle) would slide one wing or shutter out and replace it with another in order to create a new scene. The move would be almost instantaneous, and at times scene shifts received as much applause as the curtain call.

Two proscenium doors were also built for the first season in 1960. These were standard-size doors framed in rigid flats approximately six feet wide and ten feet tall, placed at a slight angle on the downstage left and downstage right sides of the stage. These doors could be used by the actors for more formal entrances, in lieu of simply entering from the wings.

Charlie Reimer went to great lengths to match the color and trim of the flats with the rest of the theatre so they would appear to be a continuation of the original structure. The front of the theatre's second tier of box seats featured a series of "medallions," many of which bore the painted profiles of some of Italy's greatest theatre artists. To complete the effect, Charlie created medallions over each of his doors: on one he painted the likeness of John Ringling, and on the other the likeness of Chick Austin.

The Baroque festival's company of actors and technicians would be made up of teachers and students, many from FSU. Art Dorlag appointed Eberle Thomas, who had acted in seminar productions and was now a graduate student at FSU, to be assistant director of the festival. Before beginning his graduate studies at his alma mater, Eb Thomas had spent three years in New York City working with the New York City Opera Company and the New York Shakespeare Festival.

Eb was able to persuade his good friend and fellow Sarasota seminar alum Robert Strane to join the acting company that first summer. Bob Strane was at that time working on a doctor of fine arts degree at Yale University.

I would not arrive in Sarasota for another season, but in the coming years and decades, I would come to know Bob quite well. The best I can do to describe him is as a somewhat eccentric person. He doted on anything Italian, spoke the language and would sing long passages from his favorite Italian operas whenever the mood struck him. He was a protégé of Yale's

A.M. Nagler, perhaps the foremost theatre historian in the United States at the time. Bob's reputation had preceded him, and the younger members of the company (myself included) tended to be somewhat intimidated by the prospect of working with someone of his stature. But Bob had ways of putting you at ease. On one occasion, barefoot on the beach, he entertained the company by impersonating one of his favorite performers: Little Richard.

The first season in 1960 opened with a double bill: Moliere's *The Ridiculous Ladies* (translated by Eb Thomas) and *The Doubles* (Eb's adaptation). This would be followed by Richard Brinsley Sheridan's *The Rivals*, Carlo Goldoni's *The Servant of Two Masters*, *The Beggars' Opera* by John Gay and George Etherege's *The Man of Mode.*

The Doubles, along with the seminar's 1953 production of *The Last Lesson of Pantalone*, was an example of *commedia dell'arte*, the Italian comedy of improvisation, a craft that "was not and could not be performed except by professional actors," wrote Pierre Louis Duchart in *The Italian Comedy*. Commedia dell'arte featured such characters as Harlequin, Pantalone and Pulcinella—the models for later centuries' circus clowns—and very much kept with Art Dorlag's idea of the Baroque style. However, considering the time required to develop such improvisational abilities, a company of student actors who would rehearse together only briefly had very little chance of pulling it off. But for their parts, the actors considered it a great adventure.

Neither the university nor the museum guaranteed that the festival would become a regular summer event, but Art Dorlag ended the first season on an optimistic note: "I am hoping that the festival will be an annual project attracting students interested in the full absorption of the Renaissance and Restoration theatre. It will be a great opportunity for background research and practical application and experience." A spark of interest had, indeed, been ignited in the community. This was important, because future seasons would almost certainly cost more than the $8,000 budgeted for the first festival.

Similar to the first season, in 1961 there were three Restoration/eighteenth-century plays, two comic operas and the commedia.

This second festival season marked my first summer with the Asolo company. Still an undergrad, I had very little experience as an actor and no knowledge whatsoever of Baroque comedies. I was there only because Eb Thomas (who had been teaching at Alabama College, now the University of Montevallo, while I was a student there) thought I owed myself "a summer of theatre" and was able to pull strings and get me into the company. (I once told Eb that he was responsible for my being in the theatre, and he, tongue in cheek, apologized.)

This season, Art Dorlag, who remained festival director, decided he would join us on stage.

The first production that summer was actually a double bill. The first half was Franz Joseph Haydn's short comic opera, *The World in the Moon*, followed after the intermission by the commedia (which had no title; most were only referred to as "scenarios"). At the start of the second part, Art would enter in a baggy Pulcinella costume, plop down on the edge of the stage and announce, "Well, you've seen Haydn, now we're gonna show you lowdn." Behind the scenes, we referred to the production as "forty magic minutes of gen-u-wine *I*-talian co-media."

It was mandatory that I be in the commedia—though this presented a special challenge to Art as the director. Not only was I inexperienced, but I also spoke with a thick southern accent. Art, then, was faced with the prospect of having someone sounding as I did attempt to participate in the Italian comedy of ad-libbing. But Art was a scholar and knew his commedia characters well. He cast me in the role of Tartalia. "He's traditionally played with a stutter or as a mute," he told me, "and I want you to play him as a mute." And so I began my pivotal first season in the theatre being told that I could make my greatest contribution by keeping my mouth shut.

Miraculously, Tartalia was a success. I found myself on stage with actors who were trying frantically to come up with funny things to say and do, and my muteness, by contrast, was a distinct advantage. It was a profound lesson in "less is more": in order to take focus, I simply had to be quiet and let simple, silent actions speak for themselves.

The Asolo Festival aspired to create a true repertory company. It was a time-honored system in Europe, albeit one fraught with complex scheduling and hard work. We actors might be cast in as many as three shows that

The playbill for the first Asolo Festival preview at FSU.

would rehearse during a five-week period, open within a two-week period and then rotate performances from day to day. The business advantage for the company was to provide opportunities for vacationing tourists to see more than one play during their stay. The additional appeal for the audience was to see the same actors perform a variety of roles in a short period of time.

For the first few seasons, we rehearsed in Tallahassee and, before moving to Sarasota, would preview one or two of the shows in FSU's Conradi Theatre. After the last Tallahassee performance, everyone in the company, from technicians to actors, would take part in striking the set and loading a truck with the scenery, props, costumes and lighting equipment that would be needed in Sarasota. The next day we'd make the drive and finally settle into the Four Seasons, an old, charming motel right on Lido Beach and just south of the Azure Tides and Three Crowns Hotels (all three have since been demolished). The hotel's owners, retired college professors, the Friedmans, were the gracious hosts and very generous with their rates: one dollar per person per day. And we could dig for clams at the south end of Lido Beach.

The first Sarasota housing for the Asolo company.

We were, in those days, a student company, receiving something like an assistantship. Some actors received college credit for the experience. For me, the solid education in period plays was invaluable.

The reviews of all the plays during those first years were almost unanimous in their praise.

The *Sarasota Scene*:

Indisputably, the best entertainment currently obtainable on the west coast of Florida is to be found in the Asolo Theatre…Before the nightly performances end some inadequately padded matron will no doubt fracture a hip while rolling in the aisles.

The *Sarasota Herald-Tribune*:

> *The festival is not merely a "first" for Sarasota, but for the entire nation. It represents a new chapter in the history of American theater.*

The local publicity for the festival and the company was superb. A formidable woman named Florence Gilmore became our energetic public relations person and regularly put together articles for the Asolo. She had no reservations about waking actors in the early hours of the morning (which was not easy—we seldom went to bed before 3 a.m.) to be photographed in all manner of "healthy" and "fun-filled" activities. One photograph that was circulated to the press showed us hand in hand in the surf with the caption, "Starting another grueling day with a refreshing dip in the gulf are these members of the Asolo Comedy Festival company." This was a typical Florence Gilmore production. But no matter how contrived, this was great exposure for the Asolo.

As an added enticement, the press releases always referred to the theatre as "the air-conditioned Asolo"—a treat for Florida audiences at the time. (Some of the un-air-conditioned shops on St. Armands Circle would even close during the warmest months.) The Ringling Museum remained open in the summer but was not air conditioned until 1963.

Local support continued to grow in the early '60s. Maas Brothers department stores began selling Asolo tickets. Demand led Asolo management to make available seventy "not the best" seats on the second and third floors. The festival had its first sold-out house in 1961 for Wycherley's *The Country Wife*. Though I only had a walk-on roll in the production (I also tried to stage manage—I was not very good at it), to have sold out a house was a cause for celebration among the company as a whole. It doesn't seem like a lot now, but at the time, we were quite pleased. And critical response remained positive. "It is not only a matter of having a summer 'culture' program," wrote the *Herald-Tribune*, "but, perhaps even more important, it is a matter of having really good entertainment available."

Still, the problem of funding loomed over plans for future summer festivals.

Art Dorlag felt that the second year was crucial; the experience of other, similar programs suggested that the festival could become self-supporting if it could survive the 1961 season. "Up to now," he said, "the program has been depending on the cooperation of the Ringling Museum and a large financial investment from FSU. But it's dubious that we can continue running a deficit operation." He surmised that neither

"Immediate and smashing success." — SARASOTA HERALD-TRIBUNE

"Funny, fast moving, ribald and filled with wit." — ORLANDO SENTINEL

THE COUNTRY WIFE
William Wycherly

THE WORLD IN THE MOON
Franz Joseph Haydn
and
COMMEDIA DELL'ARTE SCENARIO

SHE STOOPS TO CONQUER
Oliver Goldsmith

TARTUFFE
Moliere

THE SECRET MARRIAGE
Domenico Cimarosa

"Rollicking series of hilarious comedies and gay operas acted to the hilt by a top-notch company." — *Dick Bothwell*, ST. PETERSBURG TIMES.

Asolo company members took these cards into local restaurants, folded them into "tents" and placed them on each table.

the university nor the museum had adequate funds to cover the entire cost of the program, so local patrons and businesses were encouraged to increase their support.

The 1962 lineup was much the same as the first two seasons: three plays, two operas and the commedia.

In June, just as *The Way of the World* was opening the season, a group of local supporters created a financial support organization called the Asolo Theatre Festival Association. Its purpose was to "advance the cause of the theatre and to offer the public exceptional summer theatre entertainment." This organization aimed to raise money and public awareness and serve as a liaison between Tallahassee and Sarasota. In the coming year, the Association planned to promote the 1963 season opening, sell ads to finance a larger and more attractive souvenir program, provide speakers to local organizations and raise funds to underwrite the cost of opening night galas. The first president was Richard W. Cooney, a Sarasota attorney. (Not given to taking things too seriously, the actors challenged ourselves to extend the name of the organization to absurdity—"The Asolo Theatre Summer Baroque and Restoration Seminar Extravaganza," and so forth.)

On August 19, 1962, one headline read, "Asolo Festival interest is reported on upsurge." There would definitely be a fourth season.

And by that fourth season in 1963, the Asolo Theatre Festival Association would become a co-sponsor of the Asolo Festival, along with FSU and the Ringling Museum.

Art Dorlag had been convinced that an audience could be developed to provide continual support for a festival featuring the period he so loved. But during the fall of 1962, Art was forced to relinquish his position as general director of the festival because of ill health. Dick Fallon, who'd first solicited the governor on behalf of the festival, took Art's place and, after consulting with assistant directors Eb Thomas and Bob Strane, made it a priority to select plays outside of the Baroque period. The expansion of the Asolo's repertoire was the first move toward what was to be a more vibrant and ambitious future.

When Art had seen *The Country Girl* at the Asolo in 1959, he felt there was a profound incongruity between that modern play and the ambience of the eighteenth-century theatre. Years later, he still contended that the festival could have succeeded by staying with the Baroque plays and operas and that ways could have been found to increase the box office receipts, attract better talent and eventually provide a unique venue for young teachers and aspiring professionals to gain experience in that particular style.

But ironically, it was also Art who'd suggested during the 1962 season that vacationing families could be attracted by more variety. "I think a children's theatre repertory of two or perhaps three plays could have a strong assurance of success," he said, "and a musical show of the *Oklahoma* or *King and I* variety should fill the largest possible auditorium." He came back to direct shows in the 1964 and '65 seasons and continued to be listed in the program as the festival's founder.

Chapter 3

An Essential Break from the Past

In Italy, Asolo means a sunny hill town in the green ridges north of Venice. In Sarasota, it means a repertory theater of boisterous wit, free-fall nerve, unerring good taste and the daring of a cat burglar.
—Lawrence Devine, the Miami Herald

Although the repertoire was changing, the Asolo still used the Baroque-inspired wing-and-shutter scenery, and the complex shifts were still an important part of the rehearsal period. Charlie Reimer remarked that there were twelve scene changes in the 1963 production of *The Rivals*, so "there are 132 chances that someone makes a mistake." Charlie continued to spend long hours and great effort to build the scenery and props. He used 2,800 square feet of canvas that season, built period furniture and even manufactured muskets for *Cyrano*. One writer called him "historian, artist, craftsman with wood, metal, plastic and *papier-mâché*, carpenter, plumber, financial wizard and perfectionist."

The festival was becoming of growing importance to Sarasota and southwest Florida in general. The reception for the opening night of the 1963 season was held on the Ringling mansion terrace. In attendance were members of the state cabinet, legislators from Manatee and Sarasota Counties and FSU president Gordon Blackwell. A planeload of cultural and civic leaders flew in from Santo Domingo (Sarasota's sister city) for the opening of *The School for Wives*. The opening of Carlo Goldoni's *The Mistress of the Inn* was proclaimed "Italian night," and museum director Kenneth Donahue took it upon himself to telephone the mayor of Asolo, Italy, and invite him to be present. In declining, the mayor said, "We are happy to know here that the great Italian theatre tradition is being carried on in our little theatre. The theatre is like an immigrant who has attained great success in the United States and reflects glory on his native town. I thank you again and send you the liveliest wishes for the success of your undertaking."

Eberle Thomas and Pamela Payton-Wright in Goldoni's *The Mistress of the Inn*. *Photo by Evon Streetman.*

The fourth season comprised five plays (no operas or commedia), of which three were from the Baroque period. That season also included the festival's first Shakespearean production, *The Taming of the Shrew*, as well as *Cyrano de Bergerac* in a new adaptation by James Forsyth, then playwright-in-residence at London's Old Vic Theatre. The opening night of the season was standing room only, and all signs indicated that there would be many more sold-out houses. Among the actors, there was an incremental sense of excitement from one summer to the next and especially as shows from other periods were introduced into the repertoire.

The major factor in the Asolo's improving situation was Dick Fallon's energy and salesmanship. Though he remained a professor in FSU's Tallahassee-based theatre program, his dedication to Sarasota and the Asolo was unwavering. He was a producer *par excellence*, and his introduction of new styles of plays was a bold and necessary innovation. He was also responsible for a repertory schedule arranged so that all five productions could be seen in one week, or a different production on the same night for five weeks. The Asolo was catching on. On August 4, midway through the season, Dick announced that the festival's 1963 season had thus far taken in $16,000—equal to the entire income of the previous season. And by August 11, box

Anthony Ristoff, Brad Wallace and Albert Stratton in Shakespeare's *The Taming of the Shrew*. *Photo by Evon Streetman.*

office records were being broken and attendance was double that of the previous summer. Twenty-one of the fifty-eight performances in the 1963 season were standing-room only.

The reviews in 1963 continued to be positive, too. Newspapers across the state hailed the work as "brilliant," "impeccable," "not a better bet for entertainment." The Asolo Summer Festival was listed in *Life* and *Time* magazines. Joe Hayes wrote a piece for *Theatre Arts*, and another article appeared in the *National Observer*. Optimistic speculation predicted that the Asolo might develop a winter season as strong as the summer's. Dick Fallon responded, "I envision the Asolo Theatre Festival as becoming the same magnet as the Shakespearean Festivals at Stratford in Ontario and Connecticut represent."

Despite all the good news, some grumbled, even in these early years, about the Asolo's "conservative" repertoire of period plays and the lack of "cutting-edge" productions. W.C. Burnett, a local critic, quoted part of a letter he'd received from a Mrs. Rose S. Fishoff: "Unfortunately, in Sarasota, they present nothing but 16th- and 17th-century plays, usually comedies. Isn't it deplorable that no modern plays are ever presented here?" Burnett responded, "In Florida we simply haven't been able to exploit such cultural areas as yet."

Alan Schneider, a major force in the development of regional theatre, would have understood the relevance of Mrs. Fishoff's letter. He wrote in the foreword to *Regional Theatre: The Revolutionary Stage*:

> *Whenever a regional theatre sought deliberately to become regional, either in its choice of play material or in its personnel, it was too provincial or too folksy. When it wasn't doing new plays, we blamed it for timidity and conventionality. When for varying reasons and under varying pressures it started to do that and when the new plays increased in both quality and quantity, we said it was just interested in doing tryouts for New York. When companies of actors began to stick around for a season or even two at a time, we criticized the theatres for merely imitating their European antecedents or for encouraging mediocrity. When companies succumbed to casting for individual productions, we accused them of selling out to the Broadway system.*

In 1963, Mrs. Pat Howard, a graduate student at FSU, wrote a dissertation based on a survey of Asolo Festival audiences. It indicated that loyalty to the festival was of great importance: 81 percent of audience members surveyed stated that they were impressed and would return, and 50 percent attended because they felt the Asolo productions were worthwhile and stimulating. The Asolo audience had come from thirty-two different U.S. states, as well as France, Switzerland, England, Brazil, the Netherlands, Sweden, Denmark, Scotland, Venezuela, Ecuador, Italy, Guatemala, Canada and the Bahamas.

By August 1964, the fifth season was being touted as the Asolo's most successful, and a weekly Friday matinee was added to accommodate the demand for tickets.

In three years, the festival had paid more than $13,000 owed to FSU and almost doubled attendance and box office receipts. A special vacation package, offered to the summer audience, contributed to the success. With the package, participants could select one of eleven Sarasota hotels or motels to stay in for three days, see three of the festival's plays and receive dinner for two evenings from a choice of five well-known Sarasota restaurants. Additional highlights of the deal included a complimentary after-the-show drink and visits to Sarasota attractions like the Ringling Museum, Jungle Gardens and Horn's Cars of Yesterday. The total cost for two was $57.

Charlie Reimer painted fourteen portraits for the '64 production of *The School for Scandal* and modified the wing-and-shutter scenery to accommodate Shakespeare's *Twelfth Night*. That season, the Asolo produced its first modern play, Christopher Fry's *The Lady's Not for Burning*. In 1965, no Restoration or eighteenth-century play was produced; the wing-and-shutter scenery was eliminated altogether and replaced by individual sets.

In the spring of 1965, the state legislature created a five-member board, designated the State Theatre of Florida and declared the Asolo the official state theatre, whose purpose, now, would be to carry out the board's mission. Governor Haydon Burns followed this up in June by signing a proclamation declaring July and August "Asolo Theatre months" in Florida. Secretary of State Tom Adams represented the governor on the opening night of *Hamlet*, the '65 season opener, and read the proclamation, which said, in part, that the festival "has achieved increasing national and international recognition as an outstanding cultural achievement. It is particularly commendable because it gives many of our young people opportunities to develop their talent and skills in this field." Constituting an especially strong season, *Hamlet* was followed by *Volpone*, *Tiger at the Gates* and *The Importance of Being Earnest.*

During that summer of 1965, the Asolo Theatre Association announced that it had increased its membership substantially and now had members in twelve west coast Florida cities, as well as Tallahassee and Miami. The association also had formed a development committee whose purpose was to bring the festival's story to Floridians in order to stimulate fundraising and broaden the Asolo's appeal.

Major national drama editors and critics came to Sarasota for a three-day seminar, during which they saw all four productions and discussed the critic's role in regional theatre. Stuart Little of the *New York Herald Tribune*, Hobe Morrison of *Variety* and Norman Nadel of the New York *World Telegram* sat on the panel with Florida critics and representatives from the Asolo staff. Elliot Norton of the *Boston Record American* (and recipient of the George Jean Nathan Award for Dramatic Criticism) was the moderator. Norton later wrote, "The Asolo Theatre Festival is of some significance to theater goers here and throughout the country. For it is state supported, is dedicated to producing good or great plays professionally and it seems to be thriving."

Eberle Thomas's design for the 1965 production of *Hamlet*. This was the first season in which wing-and-shutter scenery was not used.

When the company arrived in Sarasota (after its Tallahassee rehearsal period) in June 1965, Sarasota mayor David Cohen, following Governor Burns's lead, read a resolution making July and August Asolo months in Sarasota. He then presented Dick Fallon with the keys to the city. Harry Schall, the new association president, gave baskets of food and other gifts to the company members—perhaps unintentionally appropriate for us starving actors.

Toward the end of August, it was estimated that more than eighteen thousand persons would attend the '65 festival. And there was more good news: the association presented another check to FSU for another chunk of the debt accrued over the years. The payment was accepted by Dr. Lawrence Chalmers Jr., dean of the College of Arts and Sciences, who then announced that the rest of the debt was forgiven: "As the Asolo Theatre Festival offers to make a partial repayment of the cumulative debt, I am pleased to announce the university has absorbed the indebtedness and will reinvest all subsequent earnings of the festival into the festival itself, both in campus preparation and subsequent seasons in Sarasota."

The numbers continued to demonstrate the Asolo's progress. In 1964, the box office revenue had been $35,000; in 1965, it was $45,000; and in 1966, it was $62,000, which was well over the $54,000 that had been budgeted. Attendance continued to grow. Before the end of the '66 season, it was predicted that twenty-two thousand people would attend the festival that year. When all was said and done, at least one full week would be standing room only.

The Asolo put together an innovative double bill for that summer of '66: a classic Greek drama in *Oedipus the King* by Sophocles, followed by Ionesco's archetype for the theatre of the absurd, *The Bald Soprano*. Amusingly, a few patrons thought that what they saw after the intermission was supposed to be the second act of *Oedipus*.

The second annual critics' seminar was held on July 15, 16 and 17, 1966. The main topic discussed was once again the drama critic's role in developing regional theatre. Norman Nadel of the *New York Telegram*, Richard Coe of the *Washington Post* and Terry Kay of the *Atlanta Journal* moderated the discussion, and many Florida critics attended.

Along with attendance and revenue, the festival continued to increase its good press, both locally and beyond.

John O. Binns, Ringling Museum board member and former director of the Sarasota Chamber of Commerce:

> *We have now become a well established summer tourist center, and I feel that much of the credit for this goes to the festival. It has helped tremendously in bringing in tourists.*

Richard Coe of the *Washington Post*:

> *Judged as a whole, as it should be, the State Theatre does Florida proud, and surely the shades of the Ringlings must be enchanted with posthumous rewards.*

Henry Hewes, writing for the *Saturday Review of Literature*:

> *Seven years ago a summer theatre festival began to put life into the playhouse for a local audience. Since then the company, under the enterprising leadership of Richard G. Fallon, has improved in quality and extended its season from 25 to 72 performances.*

Lawrence Devine of the *Miami Herald*:

> *In Italy, Asolo means a sunny hill town in the green ridges north of Venice. In Sarasota, it means a repertory theater of boisterous wit, free-fall nerve, unerring good taste and the daring of a cat burglar.*

In the wake of the '65 season's success, Dick Fallon made known his dream for the Asolo's future. He envisioned a permanent repertory company that would perform in both a summer and winter season. In the fall, the company would have a tour for high school students, at first in Florida and later nationwide. The touring plays would be connected to courses of study in the schools, aimed to bring about a greater appreciation for the theatre. Dick pointed out that such a program, which would come to be called the Educational Enrichment Tour, would be the first of its kind in the nation.

After the '66 season closed in September, U.S. representative James A. Haley (D—Florida Eighth District) announced that the Asolo would receive a federal grant from the U.S. Department of Health, Education and Welfare totaling more than $138,000. Dick, who had prepared the Asolo for the future by expanding the repertoire in 1963, had also initiated this essential funding step: he'd applied for the grant months earlier in hopes of having the funds to underwrite the fall tour of state high schools.

The new plan was for a three-pronged program: first, a high-school tour in the fall of 1966 to play in thirteen counties and before an estimated 10,500 students and 463 teachers. The schools would pay one dollar per student. Seniors would see Shakespeare's *As You Like It* and ninth graders Shaw's *Major Barbara*. (At that time, reports estimated that 90 percent of high school students in Florida had never seen a play of any kind.) Teachers would be given appropriate material beforehand, and students would read and discuss the plays before seeing them. Then students would be bused to a central location to see the productions, preceded by an informative demonstration about the theatre—all of it to be presented by the Asolo actors.

Second, the grant indirectly funded a ten week winter/spring season, including a means for advanced theatre work for FSU students.

And third, there was the regular ten-week summer season. Thus, the year would begin with the fall tour, then move on to the winter/spring season and culminate with the summer season.

One precedent for educational programs had been set years earlier during the summer of 1964, when the Asolo's house manager, Ruth Reiter (also a teacher in the Sarasota school system), took charge of eighty-five high school students who ushered, took tickets and handled other supportive jobs, like setting out the oil-burning tiki lamps that lined the narrow road to the pine-shrouded, unpaved parking lot. And those students also attended theatre seminars and could see performances of the plays more than once. The Asolo, it was said, is a place where "education meets recreation."

Student company members, circa 1964. Paul Reubens (aka PeeWee Herman) is on the far left.

It must be remembered that putting so much emphasis on education at every level kept with Chick Austin's legacy. He almost certainly would have been delighted to know that his museum and his Italian theatre were at the heart of this emphasis on education.

Dick Fallon again contacted the festival's assistant directors Eb Thomas (now in graduate school at Michigan State University) and Bob Strane (who was teaching at San Diego State in California) before the summer season of 1966 and informed them of the federal grant and the three-pronged, year-round plan. Dick told Eb and Bob that he wanted them to be the key figures in the new Asolo setup—one to be the artistic director, the other the managing director. Eb and Bob discussed the offer and decided that neither wanted to be managing director, so they made a counteroffer: they would be co–artistic directors, which would allow them also to direct and act in shows, while the festival only had to pay two salaries. According to Eb, "Dick was taken aback, but responded beautifully. He said, 'Okay, we'll make do without a managing director until next year. By then, I'll have the managing director's position included in the budget.'" As part of the arrangement, Eb and Bob also became FSU faculty members.

With the awarding of this grant, the Asolo company went from a summer festival to one functioning in all four seasons.

Association president Harry Schall reported in the '66 souvenir program that the four-year-old Asolo Theatre Association now had members in twenty-three cities throughout the state of Florida. He also listed the association's many contributions, including preparing the souvenir program and selling the ads that appeared therein. What he could not yet report, because it might have been premature, was the association's plan to renovate the old Palm Tree Playhouse (at this writing, the Gompertz Theatre) so it could be used as the Asolo's year-round rehearsal hall.

The reason we now needed a Sarasota rehearsal space was that before the '66 tour, the company had negotiated with Actors' Equity Association (the union of professional actors and stage managers) and became a union house. Immediately, the group of student actors became a company of professionals. (At the time, I was teaching speech and theatre at Southeast Missouri State College.) Michael Keenan was the Asolo's first Equity deputy and had to oversee the transition from a freewheeling system of rehearsal scheduling and management to the strictures imposed by the Equity rule book. According to Michael, this did not always sit well with Bob Strane.

The inaugural two touring shows opened at the Asolo Theatre for Manatee and Sarasota County students the second week in November 1966. Elliot Norton, writing for the *Boston Record American*, described a typical tour day, beginning with the workshop:

> *The response of the children was perfect. For one and one-half hours, they sat without so much as a murmur while the young actors of the Asolo told them how actors and actresses prepare for roles; how directors can form an ensemble; how costumes are made, settings are designed. Then, after a luncheon intermission, they watch* As You Like It *with undeviating attention and complete enthusiasm.*

Warren Cato, director of the Theatre Guild, called it "the most exciting program in theatre for secondary school children in the country."

The workshops always began with a bang. The openings were loud, energetic and zany. Our goal was to surprise and delight, and we regularly received gales of laughter and applause from the young audiences. Having gotten the students' attention, we introduced ourselves and explained why we were there. Then, before the audience could become restless, another off-the-wall demonstration began.

The demonstrations, which made legitimate points about acting and the theatre, were upgraded each season as new actors joined the workshop and added their ideas. Among the favorites was the "Dr. Frankenstein" routine, during which one actor, apparently lifeless, was brought to life by a second actor, who, through a comic building process, imbues the "monster" with the physical, vocal and intellectual/emotional abilities that are required for acting.

The "Indian routine" probably wouldn't pass today's standards for politically correctness, but it was one of the most popular and instructive demonstrations. Teachers requested that it be included in the workshop. The story involved two American Indian gentlemen who get in a fight over the affections of a lovely maiden. The dialogue was made up entirely of Florida cities and attractions that bore Indian names. For example, "Kissimmee" and "Apopka" were verbs; "Apalachicola" represented characters' laughter. The relationship between words and actions was discussed after the demonstration.

Most importantly, the touring productions weren't "kiddie shows"—watered-down classics made more palatable to high school students. (In fact, during the tours, the exact same shows were performed publicly.) The 1967 production of *Henry IV, Part One*, for example, presented Shakespeare's play without altering the time period or simplifying the characters. In one small school, the auditorium doubled as a basketball court; the stage was too small and the windows uncurtained, making the lighting effects virtually nonexistent. In short, it was a disadvantageous setting, but we plunged ahead. At the curtain call, the students erupted in a standing ovation (as happened in most schools where we played). Many students waited after the show to talk with the actors; others later wrote us letters.

No doubt, the Educational Enrichment Tour affected countless students throughout the state. Henry Hewes wrote in the *Saturday Review*, "It is in the national interest to investigate how such projects as the Florida high school tour can increase future audiences and encourage better training of talented young people in the skills of the theatre."

Following that inaugural fall tour, the Asolo Theatre's first winter/spring season opened in Sarasota on March 11, 1967, with the touring production of *As You Like It*. In the opening pages of the souvenir program, George F. Higgins, the chairman of the Ringling's board of trustees, contributed the following:

> *A museum serves its true function when it develops and sustains the living arts. One of the most lively and successful artistic ventures in the history of the Ringling Museum is the Asolo Theatre Festival…We are proud that, since its beginning, we have been—along with the Florida State University—co-sponsors of this outstanding enterprise that has contributed so greatly to the cultural life of the community and the state.*

One of the many ways the museum supported the Asolo was with the generosity it tendered on opening nights. As early as the 1963 season, the museum hosted themed opening nights that reflected the world of a given play (as mentioned, an "Italian night" for the opening of *The Mistress of the Inn*). The openings would be celebrated in this way for several years: *Twelfth Night*, which opened the summer season in 1964, had its reception on the terrace of the Ringling Mansion, and the food and music centered on an Elizabethan motif. Subsequent receptions corresponded with each play's period: seventeenth-century French for *The Imaginary Invalid*, Medieval for *The Lady's Not for Burning* and eighteenth-century English for *The School for Scandal*. The museum gave the theatre its choice of reception sites—the mansion, the courtyard or the galleries.

The reception for the first winter/spring opening in 1967 was the Asolo's most opulent. Once again the museum came forward, offering its new gallery

The opening night reception for Giradoux's *Tiger at the Gates*, 1965.

wing for the after-show ceremony. Mr. and Mrs. W.W. Johnson planned the banquet and, while working closely with the Asolo's artistic directors, managed to keep the particulars a surprise. Those attending the opening of *As You Like It* discovered a combination of Shakespeare's Forest of Arden and the then-current style of English "mod." The setting included golden draperies, torches and "interesting" (according to one newspaper) music. The catered feast included venison, chervil, roast beef, bouquet garni, baked red salmon supreme, baked ham Montmartre, whole roast suckling pig and roast turkey, *beau monde*. There was a fantastic display of salads and delicacies, as well as London desserts including apple turnovers, tarts and brownies and a "Forest of Arden" fruit table.

Despite extensive press coverage, the many talks and programs for civic groups and the gracious plenty of brochures and posters, many locals remained uncertain about the Asolo company and its new winter/spring season. The box office manager, Julian Stern, reported a "constant stream" of requests for reservations "next summer, when things quiet down a bit." The idea of an entirely new season preceding the usual summer repertory would take some time for the public to comprehend. Plus, too many patrons assumed that the "resident company" was made up of students from the FSU Theatre Department. The bios in the souvenir program were often overlooked.

At the summer season of 1967, I brought my wife of two years, Marian, to Sarasota. Though she would become the Asolo's longtime production stage manager, she began her career that summer as a box office employee.

That summer season included a premiere by playwright Mario Fratti entitled *Eleonora Duse*. It earned this accolade from local critic Lee Furman: "The Asolo Theatre Festival should be complimented in making this great step forward. It's never an easy task to produce a new play—one which has never been proven by other daring innovators. This takes courage and confidence."

Combined, the winter/spring and summer seasons would open eleven mainstage productions (which included the two touring shows)—up to that time, the greatest number ever produced in a single year. Demand dictated more opportunities to see them. Eb Thomas later confessed that he "became the dreaded Dr. Frankenstein who invented an 11-performance week"—two shows each day from Tuesday through Saturday, followed by a matinee on Sunday—up from the previous practice of nine. It was a strenuous regimen for the actors, but we were young and assumed that was the way things were supposed to be.

Henry IV, Part One, which had been so successful in front of the high school students, opened the 1968 winter/spring season to good notices. One day before opening, the national conference of resident repertory theatre directors met in the Ringling Museum. The occasion also was to honor Audrey Wood, the literary agent who had represented a host of notable American playwrights, including Tennessee Williams and William Inge. Wood was conducting a playwrights' workshop at the Asolo, and the three young writers involved—Aldo Giunta, Fred Gaines and Bill Parchman—would have a chance to showcase their work later that spring. (Gaines's play *Wilde!* was even chosen to premiere that summer as part of the repertory season.) Wood's husband and business partner, William Liebling, and her good friend Shirley Booth were also present. FSU president John Chapman read a statement from Governor Claude Kirk in which the governor acknowledged that the state's cultural activities were as important as economic and population growth.

Despite some confusion, the Asolo Theatre Festival, now in its second full season, continued to win new support and acceptance as a year-round operation. At the beginning of the '67 season (the fall tour), the box office reported that tickets for the upcoming '68 winter/spring season were selling out rapidly. (In addition to the two touring shows, that season comprised *J.B.*, *Look Back in Anger*, *Antigone* and *A Midsummer Night's Dream*.) Resident directors Bob Strane and Eb Thomas predicted that the season would be very successful.

During the spring, we were invited to go to Tallahassee to present two performances of the Thomas/Strane adaptation of Moliere's *Tartuffe*, retitled *The Preacher*, before the state legislature. Set in a border state soon after the American Civil War, this version of Tartuffe was manifest as a bearded mountain preacher; Orgon was "Mr. Organ," Elmire "Miss Elmira" and so on. A Union soldier served as the *deus ex machine* at the end of the play, while upstage, the cast hummed "The Battle Hymn of the Republic."

State legislators began the black-tie affair at FSU's Conradi Theatre, where they saw the show. Some members of that night's audience later reported that the laughter that evening sometimes reached a level that was "frightening." At a reception afterward, a number of legislators confessed that they had been "dragged" to the theatre by their wives and were surprised at how much they had enjoyed themselves. They left with a new appreciation for what the Asolo was doing.

Less than two weeks later, the Festival Association announced that it was amending its bylaws to "accommodate a year-round operation as one of the three sponsors [along with FSU and the museum] of the Asolo Theatre Festival" and that it had contracted to renovate the theatre's air-conditioning system, correct acoustical problems and improve lighting and sound systems. Before the last week of the 1968 winter/spring season, the box office reported continued sellouts. But despite what appeared to be an expanding future, storm clouds of the Asolo's first major crisis were gathering on the horizon.

Chapter 4
Hard Times

The enlargement of the human spirit is not a luxury.
—G.A. McEllan

Just seven days after the summer season's opening performance (July 20, 1968), an article in the *Sarasota Herald-Tribune* appeared with the heading, "Revenue sources sought to save Asolo Festival." Major funding of at least $250,000 a year in addition to box office revenue would be required to continue year-round operations—primarily to cover the fall Educational Enrichment Tour, which had only been guaranteed federal grants for 1966 and '67 and, to double the blow, had lost its state funding to education budget cuts. For the remainder of the summer and beyond, reports of financial problems overshadowed the festival's accomplishments and threatened to drastically change or even end what had been such a bright adventure. We were devastated.

This jumbled state of affairs apparently began with the expansion into the educational tour and the winter/spring season. When the theatre converted to a year-round company that was obligated to adhere to Actors' Equity bylaws, the annual expenses jumped from $66,000 to $440,000 in a matter of months. The deficit beyond earnings for two and a half years of operation was already $190,000, according to Dick Fallon. (The financial backing for the tour and the resident seasons were separated in ways that complicated the company's aims.) Most of the deficit was due to tour expenses. The 1968 summer season had come within $2,000 of reaching the $83,000 budgeted, and the income was well over the $61,000 taken in during the '67 season. Ironically, the increase in revenue and attendance caused the *Sarasota Herald-Tribune* to proclaim the 1968 winter/spring season as Asolo's most successful.

In an interview, Dick Fallon listed three reasons for the financial problems: One, Governor Claude Kirk and the state legislature cut appropriations for education; $46,000 for FSU and the tour were eliminated. (Eb Thomas explained that the $200,000 deficit people referred to during this period could be attributed to the "disappearance" of funds conjured by "magician" Claude Kirk.) Two, when the festival added a fall tour in 1966 and a winter/spring season in 1967, it did so with no funds for the necessary scene shop, costume shop and other essential equipment and supplies that accompanied those additional seasons. Three, with no guidelines, the festival overestimated the revenue anticipated from the first winter/spring season in 1967.

Added to this was the loss of federal funds for the tour. Only two federal grants had been promised: the $138,000 grant for the '66 tour originally had been raised to $171,000 for the '67 tour. However, the demon of red tape came into play, and the company was faulted for "misleading expenditures." The actual grant for 1967 was reduced to $140,000.

Rumors and misinformation complicated matters further. Dick Fallon acknowledged that the festival had suffered from an image problem, that too many people thought of the Asolo as a "highbrow" or "society" enterprise. On the other hand, there was still confusion about the company's composition. One letter to the editor complained, "For a theater company like the college group from Tallahassee (which calls itself the Asolo Drama Festival) to have incurred a working deficit of $135,000...is fiscal infamy." Fallon wrote a response letter and patiently corrected the writer. In the *Sarasota Herald-Tribune* on July 6, 1968, the headline read: "Asolo Theatre's future termed cloudy; fall tour set, but beyond that...??"

There was some talk about moving the company to another Florida city, possibly Palm Beach, if Sarasota could not support the year-round operation. (Although according to some insiders, this rumor may have been a ruse on the part of a handful of Asolo authorities to draw attention to the situation.)

The *Sarasota Herald-Tribune* reported on September 30, 1968: "FSU budget hit by regents. An estimated $190,000 deficit in FSU's budget connection with the famed Asolo Theatre of Sarasota drew fire Friday from a Board of Regents member...A regents spokesman said the deficit occurred when federal funds expected to help cover the cost did not come. The Board of Regents has already prohibited FSU to allow any further debts."

The board, upset by the confusing reports, threatened to audit the Asolo's books.

Two plays with relatively small casts (Shaw's *Arms and the Man* and Moliere's *The Misanthrope*) had been chosen for the '68 fall tour; but when Eb Thomas called me about casting, he included a caveat: "We want you in the touring company this fall—if there is a company." Other prospective cast members received the same warning. And when the tour did commence, the business manager warned us that each paycheck could be our last.

During the summer of 1968, Dick Fallon and the Asolo management made a move that would affect the Asolo's future more than anyone could have imagined: they hired Howard J. Millman as the Asolo's first managing director.

Howard was Dick's student at Hartwick College in Oneonta, New York, twenty years earlier. From Hartwick, Howard had gone to Purdue University, where he received his MA in theatre in 1953. Immediately prior to coming to FSU, where he'd planned to work on a PhD, Howard had been the civilian director of the theatre and entertainment division at Fort Bragg, North Carolina.

When he arrived in Sarasota in July 1968, Howard was greeted with a hug from Dick Fallon. "I'm so glad you're here," said Dick. "We're $250,000 in debt and may not open our doors in the fall." (The Asolo Theatre Association at that time had $12,000 in the bank.) Undaunted, Howard accepted the job but asked for two major considerations. First, he wanted to continue to have the opportunity to direct shows.

The second request was more complicated. Dick, who now held the title of Asolo executive director, also remained the general director of the Theatre Department at FSU and was therefore required to be in Tallahassee much of the time. Howard asked for assurance that he wouldn't have his decisions overruled at "long distance." Dick agreed to both conditions and promised to devote his efforts "to the growth of the state theatre as a cultural, educational, and economic force on Florida's west coast." Howard would be the hands-on, day-to-day managing director of the Asolo. His starting salary was $9,600, with some extra for the summer.

Howard knew that he'd stepped into the middle of a quagmire. After conferring with Dick, he agreed that it was of tremendous importance to keep the touring program going, that it would be a mistake to lose the momentum of a fall season and the prospect of some money coming in the spring and summer. Still, he was handicapped by his lack of experience with the tour, so he turned to Dan Parr, the Asolo's former director of instruction, who had booked the first two touring seasons.

Dan held the position from the summer of 1966 to the fall of 1968. During that short time, he created a crucial educational summer program that brought in high school and college students to take classes in acting, directing, design and research projects. But in 1968 he'd left Sarasota and returned to FSU to complete work on a doctorate. Fortunately, he was still available.

Dan contacted major newspapers in cities the Asolo hoped to tour and asked them to be local sponsors. The response was generous and enthusiastic. Some papers—the *Daytona Beach News-Journal*, for example—gave money, while others contributed free advertising for the evening public performances. The *Miami Herald*'s coverage was so successful that patrons had to be turned away from the Coconut Grove Playhouse, where we were performing. With this aid and the support of civic organizations and individuals, the tour was able to complete its 1968 run. Before Christmas, newspapers were able to publish the lineup of plays in the winter/spring season, which included *The Hostage*, *The Homecoming*, *Uncle Vanya* and *Two Gentlemen of Verona*. The latter was staged as an American western, with the appropriate ten-gallon hats and six-shooters. (I played Launce as a Chinese houseboy; company member Bill Pitts played my dog, Crab.) The Asolo's year-round program had survived—at least, for the time being.

FSU helped the cause when, in the fall of 1968, FSU president John Champion erased the deficit using money from his discretionary fund (known as "the Coke fund," because it came from the sale of soft drinks at the university).

Though the company was still not out of the woods financially, what had been the adolescent Asolo was now showing signs of fiscal maturity and self-reliance.

Early in the year, FSU had withdrawn as the Asolo's corporate entity, making it necessary for a new corporation, the Asolo State Theatre Inc., to take responsibility for the Asolo's operation. As regards the theatre's recent financial crisis, Dick Fallon wrote, "The fate of the Asolo's continuation hung in the balance. The State Board of Regents and Florida State University responded in a way that must always be remembered by those who cherish the Asolo."

The new corporation's board of directors held an organizational meeting at the Southgate branch of the First Federal Savings and Loan and created a nominating committee to select a number of Sarasota and Bradenton residents for the board of directors. Sometime later there was a very important gathering at the home of Maurice Hirsch, a notable supporter of the arts in Sarasota. (Hirsch's daughter, Carolyn Michel, would become a prominent Asolo actress in the coming decades—and, eventually, Howard Millman's wife.) As a result of that meeting, Hirsch became instrumental in clearing the way for the corporation's 501c3 not-for-profit status.

In January 1969, the Governor's Conference on the Arts met at the Asolo Theatre to discuss the "economic value of cultural development." The conference brought together nationally recognized business and arts leaders and stressed the need for greater involvement in the arts by business, government and individuals. Dick Fallon acted as moderator.

Among the arts leaders were George G.R. Harris of the Stratford Shakespearean Festival, Ontario, and W. Howard Adams, director of national programs for the National Gallery of Art. Business was represented by Arthur L. Harris, president of Scripto Inc.; Everett O. Jones, divisional manager of Container Corporation of America; and George M. Irwin, chairman of the board for the Quincy Compressor Division of Colt Industries Inc. G.A. McEllan, president of the Business Committee for the Arts, Inc., disputed the notion that the place of art was in any way secondary. "Neither education nor technology will save society," he said. "The enlargement of the human spirit is not a luxury."

The participants emphasized that corporations needed to help arts groups effectively manage their own programs. To this end, it was suggested that "corporations could not only contribute money, but could also support the arts with their own people who had special talents and experience in the management field."

The recommendations made during the Governor's Conference caught the attention of the Sarasota community. In April, Adolph "Chick" Frankel (who would soon become president of the Asolo Theatre Festival Association) brought together local bankers and businessmen for the purpose of coming to grips with what would almost certainly be ongoing deficits. As a regional theatre, the Asolo had a certain responsibility to make the plays affordable to the audience, so raising ticket prices beyond a certain point was not an option. The theatre's small size (312 seats) imposed further limits. FSU would continue to pay the salaries of Eb Thomas, Bob Strane, Howard Millman and the resident set designer, Holmes Easley, but production costs and the remainder of the company—actors, technicians, management staff—would have to be covered by something beyond box office revenue. Frankel made this point to the group and reminded them that it would be an economic as well as a cultural loss if the Asolo should have to close.

The meeting resulted in what came to be called the Asolo's Business Advisory Committee. William C. Coleman, president of Palmer First National Bank and Trust of Sarasota, was named chairman. The committee, which would work in conjunction with the association's fundraising efforts, made deficit reduction its primary function. It was prepared to raise as much as $25,000 to underwrite anticipated deficits. "Perhaps the most significant accomplishment of this entire effort," Coleman wrote, "was the restoration of mutual confidence between the acting company, the Festival Association and the business community. Each now recognizes the importance of the others to its own well being. Hopefully, this may be the beginning of a new era of strength and growth for the Asolo and a further enrichment of Sarasota business and cultural life." Dick Fallon proudly noted, "This group has put us in contact with the business community for the first time."

The Asolo Theatre Festival Association had laid the groundwork for this kind of support by tripling its membership and joining the museum and FSU as sponsors of the year-round Asolo. In 1969, there began a "drastically revamped promotional program" to further strengthen the Asolo's foundation. It was during this time that two of the Asolo's most important supporters, Chick Frankel and Bettilu Lewis, came up with the nickname "Asolo Angels" for the members of the association. Traditionally in the theatre, "angels" are backers who finance a new production. Here, of course, the definition was much broader, as the association members not only donated money but also volunteered their time and expertise to underwrite the theatre's success. Chick Frankel opined in the souvenir program, "Probably no other theatre in the country has so many experts working for it without pay."

The Asolo moved ahead in 1969 by making a substantial change in its scheduling. The three separate seasons (fall, winter/spring and summer) each had been divided by a rehearsal period during which the theatre had no productions running. In April, Howard Millman received permission from the Ringling Museum trustees to perform in the theatre from May 11 to June 19—a time that ordinarily would have been for rehearsals only. Two particularly popular winter/spring shows—*The Lion in Winter* and *Oh What a Lovely War*—were chosen to continue their run into June. While these two shows were playing, the summer shows were in rehearsal. This new, unbroken season extended from February to Labor Day and would be the rule for some years to come.

This new schedule was not just a boon for audiences. A continuous season gave continuous employment, which was a good thing for actors who were still developing their careers.

Tom Prideaux, theatre editor of *Life* magazine, lectured for a Sunday afternoon program in July. Prideaux praised the Asolo company and the productions in glowing terms. The faithful Henry Hewes had visited again and written yet another article for the *Saturday Review* in which he predicted a successful future for the Asolo. The optimism of the critics was well founded: the summer season in 1969 was going well, and the box office receipts for the winter/spring season had been 55 percent over the previous year with an average of more than two hundred admissions per performance. The 1969 season was being hailed, as Hewes put it, as "the most popular of any to date."

Chapter 5

Education and Politics

The Asolo tour is only one of the many ways Florida's official state theatre company makes sure that this state's children will not grow up without the true education that theatre offers.
—*Richard Stone*

The early 1970s saw the Asolo achieve new standards of quality in both its mainstage productions and its educational programs—this in spite of a constant battle to stabilize the budget.

The 1970 souvenir program announced yet another innovation: co-production. "Theatre devotees who wish to become intimately and actively involved with the professional troupe may now contract to underwrite the staging of specific plays throughout the year, based on budgeted figures available to the Asolo management."

That season opened on February 19, with a production of Noel Coward's *Blithe Spirit.* The next night saw the opening of Tennessee William's *The Glass Menagerie,* which was co-produced by Audrey Wood, in memory of her now late husband, William Liebling. Along with her husband, Wood, the literary agent who'd hosted a playwrights' workshop at the Asolo two years earlier, represented Tennessee Williams from 1937 to 1954. The couple had also been active supporters of the Asolo. In presenting her gift, Wood said, "I can think of no memorial which would have pleased Liebling more—supporting one of Tennessee's plays as performed by the Asolo's fine company."

The Asolo didn't shy away from technically daunting productions that demanded considerable effort from the stage crew. A new adaptation of *Dr. Faustus* in 1970 was the most complex show the Asolo had produced to date.

The set included the installation of a grated floor that allowed actors to be lit from below and a large swing that "flew" Faustus and Mephistopheles "across the world" and over the first few rows of seats in the orchestra. Actors sometimes volunteered to help the overworked crew strike the set after the curtain call. (In rotating repertory, the sets were set up before and taken down after each performance.) Robert Strane directed.

...Not that our technical ambitions always went smoothly. During one performance of *Dr. Faustus*, I, as Gluttony, waited backstage for an entrance alongside the six other Deadly Sins. Moments before we were to go onstage, I looked over to see Wrath, who often got caught in the set's massive revolving door, furiously trimming pieces from his costume to make the entrance easier.

Dan Parr, who had been such a great aide to Howard Millman during the crisis of '68, left a solid foundation for the next director of instruction, Jon Spelman, to build on.

In February 1969, Jon introduced three summer educational programs: a student company made up of college seniors and graduate students; an apprentice company made up of college sophomores and selected freshmen; and a three-week seminar for secondary school teachers. Academic credit was awarded through FSU, which now had the largest theatre program in the Southeast. By June 1971, fifty-nine young people from eighteen states had arrived in Sarasota to begin their work at the Asolo.

Jon regarded the summer programs as an important educational experience for the students. They performed small roles and worked with the technical crews, attended classes, seminars and workshops and learned the nuts and bolts of making costumes, painting scenery and welcoming patrons to each performance.

In addition to these new learning programs, the Educational Enrichment Tour went on the road for the fifth consecutive year in 1970. In the previous four years, seven different plays had been presented to eighty thousand students, three thousand teachers and thirty-four thousand people who had attended the public performances. Despite its great success, however, the problem of funding persisted. For the present, the tour survived without federal funds.

The high school–bound Educational Enrichment Tour extended to an elementary counterpart, the Children's Theatre program. Dr. Moses Goldberg, who had degrees in both child psychology and theatre, was the director of Children's Theatre at FSU and a guest director for the Asolo during the summer and fall of 1970. That summer he organized a production of *The Tortoise and the Hare* using the high school and college students from the summer program. (Richard Hopkins, who would go on to be one of the leaders in Sarasota's theatre scene, played the Hare.) That fall, advanced students from FSU participated in the Asolo's first statewide tour for elementary students. "It's not just for children," Dr. Goldberg said. "Families should come together. It should be a sharing."

During the fall of 1970, the Asolo Theatre was placed by legislative act under the Cultural Affairs Office of the Florida secretary of state. For the first time, funds could come directly from the state, and help for the 1971–72 seasons had already been requested. It also was announced that the Asolo would be one of only twenty-six resident professional theatres to receive grants from the National Endowment for the Arts. The grant, made through the Asolo Theatre Festival Association, was for $12,500 and was intended for the production of new plays, staff enlargement, extended educational and community services, audience development, regional touring and training programs. Fred Wright of the *St. Petersburg Independent* wrote, "For the first year, then, the Asolo apparently will be out of the red, if pledges toward the subsidy are met…Howard Millman is increasingly confident that the darkest days are over."

The Asolo's box office sales through the winter of 1970–71 were $40,000 better than the stellar 1968–69 season. Howard listed several reasons for the current success, including substantial preseason subscription sales, new and efficient publicity, increased community support and a choice of plays that proved to be popular: that season; we performed *Born Yesterday*, *Our Town*, *Indians* and *The Comedy of Errors.* I also directed the latter, setting it as an homage to *Laugh-In*—using a psychedelic set and a soundtrack that included the likes of Spike Jones.

In praising the increased ticket sales, one headline read, "The Sweet Smell of Success." But in May 1971, the Florida state legislature, just one year after being put in a position to give direct aid to the Asolo, cut the theatre's allocation from the state budget. The financial roller coaster ride continued.

Despite the efforts of State Representatives Robert M. Johnson and Granville H. Crabtree Jr. and state senate president pro tempore William Boyd, the funds for the Asolo had been removed from a budget bill being considered by a joint conference committee. "Legislators have chosen this non-election year to get tough with appropriations," wrote Dick Bloom of the *Herald-Tribune.* "Projects such as provided by the Asolo…have been described by some legislators as 'Dancing in the streets.'" Dick Fallon told legislators he needed a subsidy of $40,000 and had overdue bills of $25,000.

Secretary of State Richard Stone, who would prove to be a faithful and energetic friend to the Asolo, refused to give up. Stone put $80,000 for the Asolo in his first budget proposal, allocating the funds primarily to the touring programs. Stone explained, "The Asolo tour is only one of the many ways Florida's official state theatre company makes sure that this state's children will not grow up without the true education that theatre offers." But Governor Reubin Askew's budget bureau refused to consider any financial help for the Asolo.

Secretary Stone's next move was to ask the cabinet for $20,000 in emergency funds. The money being sought could be allocated by the Fine Arts Council (of which Chick Frankel was a member and Asolo's old friend, Tippen Davidson, publisher of the *Daytona Beach News-Journal*, was president). The council served as an advisory body to Stone and the Division of Cultural Affairs. But even if the proposal should get a majority vote from the cabinet, it still could be vetoed by the governor.

Headlines from June 28, 1971, include: *Tampa Times*, "Cabinet asked to rescue Asolo"; *Lake Wales Highlander*, "Wolf's at door of Asolo, Stone asks for theater help"; *Tampa Tribune*, "State's Asolo Theatre may be facing its final curtain"; and *Florida Times-Union*, "Asolo Theatre may close if cabinet refuses funds."

On June 29, the state cabinet approved a transfer of $20,000 from the emergency fund for the Asolo Theatre. The Fine Arts Council was unanimous in its support, and there was no veto. Bettilu Lewis, now executive secretary of the Asolo Angels, said, "This release of funds establishes a precedent. Not only will the money help us get in the black for this operational year…but will also put us on sound footing for future requests." Secretary Stone traveled to Sarasota to deliver the money in person. The $20,000 was matched by a federal grant, and local residents had already raised $35,000 toward operations for the coming year. Once again, the Asolo dodged a bullet.

There was more good news. On July 25, Jon Spelman announced the receipt of a $2,000 grant from the John Golden Fund in New York for the Asolo's educational programs. The Golden Fund was a national foundation to help theatres and other performing arts groups. It was hoped that this recognition would prompt a similar response from other foundations. Also, Secretary Stone announced early in 1972 that $60,000 would go to the Asolo to fund the Educational Enrichment Tour. "This is the first time a direct legislative appropriation has been given to a state fine arts program [direct *legislative* appropriation as opposed to the cabinet's earlier $20,000 transfer]," noted Stone. "It sets a precedent from which to work in the next session."

The "Mr. G. French" logo.

Eugene Berman's logo.

The early Asolo celebrated the Restoration and eighteenth-century theatre, and so it was only natural that a logo for the festival evolve from that period. The comic character of Harlequin stemmed from Arlecchino, a stock character in the commedia dell'arte. On the first-floor walls of the museum's Asolo wing were displayed fifteen rare paintings by the eighteenth-century artist Giovanni Domenico Ferretti, all displaying Harlequin in various disguises and pursuits. There developed a natural bond between the Harlequin figure and the Asolo.

In the Harlequin's first appearance as a logo of sorts for the Asolo, ad materials for the 1961 season featured an early nineteenth-century print found in the Ringling Museum of the Circus. The caption identified "Mr. G. French" as the actor in the print. In 1964, Eugene Berman, who had designed the set for the Asolo's opening night in the Ringling Museum's gallery 21, created an image that would be used for the next four years.

But what would become the Asolo's most recognizable logo was a variation of a Harlequin collage by local artist Harrison Covington; it first appeared on the cover of the 1968 souvenir program. In the same spirit, beginning in the winter of 1971, local artists were invited to create a cover image for each show—a painting, pen-and-ink, collage, etc.—that would capture the essence of a particular production and then be reproduced in the souvenir program. Thorton Utz, Ben Stahl and Syd Solomon were among the many local artists who contributed to this project. These works were later auctioned, and a percentage of the proceeds went to the Asolo—a generous tradition on the artists' part that continued for the next three seasons.

The 1972 season was mercifully uneventful, insofar as financial crises were concerned. The Business Committee became the "Board of Directors of the Asolo State Theatre, Inc." Word reached Sarasota that a reproduction of the Asolo Theatre was to be constructed in its original setting, Queen Catherine Cornaro's palace in Asolo, Italy. In his book, *How to Succeed Far Off Broadway*, William Glover, drama critic for the Associated Press, wrote, "As everyone from the Keys to Pensacola knows, Asolo… is Florida's official state theater, and an exceptional example of regional dramatic enterprise."

Though it may be a bit difficult to imagine on a stage with only a twenty-eight-foot proscenium opening, in 1972 the Asolo presented the Piscator adaptation of the epic *War and Peace*, directed by Eb Thomas. It was hailed as a stupendous success. Local critic Martin Shartar wrote, "The current production of *War and Peace* preserves a surprising amount of the novel's content…and the production is so good that on its own terms the evening is by turns powerful, moving and totally engrossing."

Harrison Covington's Harlequin. The original collage was 48 inches by 48 inches.

The Asolo production of *War and Peace*, adapted by Erwin Piscator.

Actors-in-the-Schools: Brad Wallace, Richard Hopkins and Penelope Willis in Chekov's *The Marriage Proposal.*

Howard Millman said, "I think it is going to be one of the most memorable productions the Asolo has had." He was right.

That fall, Richard Hopkins, Penny Willis and I created a new educational touring program, Actors-in-the-Schools. Based on the same format as the still successful Educational Enrichment Tour (and inspired by the continued demand it generated), Actors/Schools was an endeavor to bring an in-depth look at theatre by going into the high schools rather than having students bused to a central location. The most important aspects of the program were the classes, but there were also stage performances for the entire student body, teacher workshops and sessions with students who had some interest in pursuing a career in the theatre.

This was also the year the Ford Foundation began giving "stability grants" to certain regional theatres. When the Asolo didn't receive one, Howard Millman called the foundation. The conversation, he says, went like this:

Millman: "How come these other theatres got the money and we didn't?"

Ford: "Because you didn't ask."

Millman: "So now I'm asking."

The Asolo was awarded a grant.

This was not just a handout but a complex "realistically conceived schedule of financial assistance and incentives" that required a comparable response from the theatre and its supporters. The grant would provide $60,000 at the beginning of each year for three years to be used as working capital. If the Asolo could raise $60,000 during each of the three years, by the end of the third year it would have built a cash reserve of $180,000. Chick Frankel hailed the Ford Grant as the most important honor yet bestowed upon the Asolo, which was one of only ten American theatres (and the only one in the Southeast) to receive such recognition.

The awarding of the grant had a significant effect on the community. Many city leaders and businessmen who before thought the Asolo was run by a group of addle-minded college professors now saw the festival as a legitimate undertaking that deserved their support.

Also in the mid-'70s, Sarasota County announced plans to appropriate $60,000 to upgrade the city's Payne Park for the benefit of the Chicago White Sox. Howard Millman formed the Sarasota Professional Arts Alliance and, at a county meeting, packed the house with Asolo supporters. "You're giving $60,000 to a for-profit organization because it brings people into town for a brief period in the spring," they said. "Consider

Barbara Reid, Isa Thomas and Walter Rhodes in Rick Beyosan's *Little Mary Sunshine*, 1973.

Conservatory students in the 1975 mainstage production of *Guys and Dolls* by Frank Loesser.

what the arts community does year-round." The county agreed, and the Arts Alliance also got a grant of $60,000—a part of which, of course, went to the Asolo.

Hearkening back to the early years of the commedia, the Asolo took another creative gamble in 1973. Few of us in the acting company claimed to be singers or dancers; nevertheless, we were cast in the musical *Little Mary Sunshine*. This, as with all the shows big and small, was part of the rotating repertory. Although the show produced a great deal of anxiety in the acting company, the effort was successful and would be followed with equal success by musical greats like *Guys and Dolls* and *The Music Man*. The public approved; the houses were packed.

Eb Thomas resigned his position in 1973, making Bob Strane the sole artistic director. Bob Strane and Howard Millman wore their passions for the theatre and the success of the Asolo on their sleeves. The two openly expressed very strong opinions about what course the Asolo should take, and this often led to heated disagreements. But that passion also became the basis for a remarkable and successful collaboration and ultimately a lifelong friendship.

The Palm Tree Playhouse in downtown Sarasota had long been considered for a rehearsal hall; as far back as 1966, the association had set its sights on restoring it. But stopgap repairs only lasted so long, and by the '70s the building was so dilapidated (at least one person had fallen through the floor) that it was considered unsafe. At this point, the cost of renovation would have been prohibitive. But we still needed a rehearsal space.

For almost two years in the early '70s, we Asolo "gypsies" wandered about Sarasota in search of a permanent place to stage our shows. An empty house near Sarasota Jungle Gardens was used for a brief time; rehearsals were frequently interrupted by screaming peacocks. We rehearsed in storefronts at Trail Plaza and Hillview Street near Sarasota Memorial Hospital, a YMCA near Twenty-seventh Street and Lockwood Ridge Road and a classroom at Booker High School for one summer season.

Arguably the most memorable rehearsal space was on the corner of Lemon Avenue and Main Street in downtown Sarasota: the former Get Together Club, a large room painted a depressing purple and still projecting the aura of a psychedelic gathering place. Rehearsing comedy there demanded some deal of concentration. (In the '80s, the space became a Burger King; as of this writing, it houses a Brooks Brothers clothing store.)

Finally, the Asolo Association rented a large, two-story building located on the eastern side of the Sarasota airport and once owned by the Mercury Outboard Motor Company. For the next twenty-eight years, the Mercury building would be home to a rehearsal hall, a costume shop with costume storage, a "campus" for the growing graduate program and, in time, a second theatre.

For our parts, we company members quickly became fascinated by a warehouse-like space on the building's southwest corner. Through a second-floor window, we watched as World War II P51 Mustang fighters were restored and test flown. Rumor had it that the airplanes were being sold to various Central American governments.

The Mercury building was owned by Brunswick Corp. of Skokie, Illinois. In early 1973, the company had arranged to sell the property to Latco Utilities, Inc., which caused Asolo officials to exercise their thirty-day option and right of first refusal. The association formed a syndicate and tried to raise money to purchase the building. They were still thousands of dollars short just days before the option would expire. Then, in the tradition of generosity that had kept the Asolo alive, local residents Mr. and Mrs. Joseph Penner decided to buy the Mercury and rent it to the Asolo. "It seems ridiculous for local people to have to do the financing for an institution of the state of Florida," said one Sarasota County commissioner. Howard Millman, who had first spoken to the Penners about the Asolo's problem, couldn't thank them enough.

After Chick Frankel passed away in 1975, the Mercury was renamed the Frankel Building in honor of one of the Asolo's most devoted supporters. Frankel had become president of the Asolo Theatre Association in 1969 after retiring from an executive position at Westinghouse, where he'd participated in the Manhattan Project during World War II. Also in 1969, he was appointed to the fifteen-member Fine Arts Council of Florida, which met regularly to "advise the Secretary of State on programs designed to stimulate and encourage, throughout the state, the study and presentation of the performing and visual arts." On the opening night of the 1970 season, Frankel received an ovation from the audience when the souvenir program was dedicated to him. The opening page stated, "The Asolo State Theatre Company with its heartfelt appreciation dedicates this book to Adolf 'Chick' Frankel without whose brilliance and dedicated support this stage would be silent tonight."

In addition to rehearsal spaces, the Asolo had attempted to find a space to develop new work and present cutting-edge plays. The Palm Tree Playhouse, which had been purchased from the Asolo and renovated by Anita Katzman before being loaned back to the theatre, became the Asolo's "Stage Two," opening with Jules Feiffer's *Knock Knock* on November 24, 1976, starring David Howard and me. On November 17, 1978, hindered by a lack of attendance, Stage Two opened its third and final season with the first ever production of Maga William's *In This Golden Land.*

Another attempt at a second stage would occur in January 1986, when the Asolo opened "Stage Too" in the Frankel Building with David Mamet's *A Life in the Theatre*. That performance space closed after one season. Nobody could find the building.

The lack of long-term success for these second stages can be attributed to more than one factor. There weren't enough parking spaces at downtown Sarasota's Palm Tree Playhouse, and patrons had difficulty finding the Frankel Building. But surely a major problem was one of proximity. The Palm Tree Stage Two was no more than a city block from the nascent Florida Studio Theatre and may well have been thought to be FST's offspring, not the Asolo's. The Frankel was a large, cold structure, so strikingly different from the jewel box first stage that theatregoers would have been hard-pressed to associate it with the Asolo.

These experiences lead me to argue that second theatres, which are essential to a regional theatre so that it can workshop new plays and do experimental work, should be so located that their tie to the mainstage cannot be confused.

Chapter 6

More Innovation

If you want something at this theatre, no matter how unusual or tricky it is, you should ask for it. I never feel that anything is too much to ask in terms of ingenuity.
—Bob Strane

Florida State's master of fine arts degree in theatre had been associated with the Asolo for several years, and until 1973, students had been required to spend only a year on the Sarasota "campus." Beginning that fall, the entire two-year program was transferred to the Asolo. Dr. Bernard Engel was chosen as the first director of acting (he also was made professor of acting at FSU). He had received an MFA degree at the Yale Drama School and a PhD at the University of Pittsburgh and was, at the time of his hire, teaching at the University of Alberta in Canada. Rooted in hard work, Bernie's vision for the program's structure and content established a pioneering foundation that allowed the conservatory to flourish. He related his story to me in a letter in August 2004. It began in Edmonton, Alberta, Canada, in February 1973.

> *My wife* [Bette Oliver, who would become a much-beloved actress in the Asolo's resident company] *drove me to the airport in a blizzard. Mary Corrigan* [soon to be the program's director of voice production], *unknown to me at the time, happened to be on the same flight. Howard introduced us to one another and we drove to St. Armands Key for a bite to eat.*
>
> *I believe we were the right people in the right place at the right time. We found ourselves thrown together in a crucible of unique and extraordinary circumstances: A. Sarasota, essentially an upper-income retirement enclave,*

dedicated time and philanthropy in support of cultural endeavors for the enlightenment of the community. B. A graduate acting program to be integrated with a professional repertory theatre, essentially a self-governing satellite of Florida State University in association with the state legislature and the Ringling Museum. C. [The opportunity] *to create a professional training program on the European model (studio training completely integrated with a mature ensemble of professionals), working virtually year-round presenting a full spectrum of dramatic literature in revolving repertory.*

"Revolving repertory" was the model and key dimension that would govern the design for the curriculum. Revolving repertory directly opposes the "star system." Revolving repertory directly demands versatile actors who can assume many characters, back-to-back, during the long season. The classroom, therefore, must concentrate on training a flexible "instrument" (body, voice, speech, a creative and analytical mind) that can play many tunes. But the classroom is merely the beginning. By extension, playing a myriad of roles in repertory continues and deepens education for life, moving the students from apprentice to intern to journeyman to master craftsman to artisan to artist. To augment instruction and training requirements, Howard's budget guaranteed funding for bringing in auxiliary instructors throughout that first year. Jimmy Hoskins was often engaged as choreographer for the Asolo's musical productions. When Jimmy was in residence, he willingly gave his time and talents to work within the program.

To weave students more closely into the tight-knit ensemble fabric of the Asolo company, the understudy system was suggested and readily accepted by Bob [Strane]. *In a very real sense then, professional actors in the company became valued mentors.*

An understudy performance was scheduled for 9:00 in the morning before the matinee of the same show. I believe it was Howard who suggested that we open these to the general public free of charge. Howard knew his community! As the word spread, incredibly, there would be a line of patrons, 9:00 in the morning, streaming into the theatre to see an understudy performance of King Lear *(for example).*

CLASSES (times approximate)
Classes would be held 6 days in the week:
8:00—Mary began the day with one hour of physical and vocal warm-up.
9:00–10:00—Voice and speech with Mary.
10:00–12:00—Movement and dance with Jimmy Hoskins (when in residence).

Bernard Engel in the 1980 production of *Idiot's Delight* by Robert E. Sherwood. *Photo by Gary W. Sweetman.*

1:00–5:00—Acting techniques with me (or guest instructor).
7:00–11:00—Perform minor and supporting roles as assigned in the repertory, attend rehearsals as cast or members and/or understudies.

[A student] *held up her hand in class one day to ask, "Can you schedule a time for me to wash my hair?"*

The end-of-term project [for the students' first year] *was to be a modern classic in "heightened" language, with characters that demand careful study and preparation in every particular, offering challenges in movement, gesture, voice, speech, and character analysis in depth.*

[The second year thesis project:] *Students would be required to research and write a one-person performance that would hold the stage for approximately 40 minutes. This* mis-en-scene *requires scholarly research, playwriting, dramaturgy, costuming, set decoration (if not design), coaching and directing.*

For season patrons, then, the opportunity to see that student in a solo recital following the evening performance was like enjoying a sweet dessert after the main fare.

Bob, Howard, Mary and I traveled to Tallahassee several times during the academic year to meet with Dick [Fallon] *and the campus-bound*

> *faculty. I believe those meetings were an attempt on Dick's part to keep some unity and integrity in his otherwise bifurcated faculty. But I believe those meetings were completely unnecessary and a waste of time and energy. The Asolo contingent had little or nothing in common with their campus colleagues. We were not on the same academic schedule as Tallahassee. They could do nothing for us. We could do nothing for them.*

So frustrated with this situation, Bernie Engel left the Asolo after the 1975 season to pursue more work as an actor and director. He returned in the summer of 1980 as a member of the acting company and played the leading role in *Idiot's Delight* and Mendoza in *Man and Superman*.

Bernie Engel's academic innovation at the time was mirrored in the accomplishments of the Asolo's behind-the-scenes technicians. In 1974, Martin Petlock, the Asolo's lighting designer, wrote an article in which he explained in some detail how the non-acting company went about creating on-stage magic.

Theatres divide the non-acting staff into two areas, he explained: front of house, which included management, publicity, house management, secretarial staff, ticket sales and ushers; and back of house, which included grips (stagehands), property, shop and wardrobe crews, design staff, technical director and those who handle the sound and lighting equipment. The back-of-house technicians were further divided into a production crew, which created and gathered all the scenic and sound elements for a production, and the run crew, which oversaw every performance. When Marty Petlock's article was written, there were forty non-actors necessary to support an acting company of fourteen.

Prior to each production's rehearsal period, the director outlined his ideas for the production with all those who would be involved. There were face-to-face discussions with the key personnel—designers and technicians—who presented their ideas and tried to impose a reality check on the director's aspirations. In time (hopefully), there would be a meeting of the minds, and the actual creation of the play's visual and auditory world could move forward.

Marty wrote, "The set is turned over to the kingpin of backstage Asolo: Mr. Victor Meyrich. Vic's job is simple. He decides how to make it, who will do it and when and where, how many people it will take to move it, when it will go into the theatre, and most important, will it fit on the Asolo stage."

Before coming to the Asolo, Victor Meyrich had worked for Ellis Rabb at the Association of Producing Artists (APA), for Bill Ball at the American

Conservatory Theater (ACT) and for Joseph Papp at the New York Shakespeare Festival. He also had been the technical director for the California Institute of Repertory Theater and the Front Street Theater in Memphis. He arrived in Sarasota on January 1, 1969, and, he said, "found nothing." The shop's worktables had been cut up and used to make the set for the 1968 touring show, *Arms and the Man*, and there was a decided lack of power tools. The entire budget for the shop in the coming year was $1,300. Vic informed Howard Millman that the entire $1,300 would be used to update the shop's equipment. The rest of the budget, he said, could be discussed later.

Victor Meyrich, Asolo production manager. *Photo by Gary W. Sweetman.*

It should be remembered that these sets were built for rotating repertory, which meant that they had to be extremely sturdy and designed so that they could be quickly disassembled and stored. Sets for the next performance (sometimes later in the same day) must then be brought on stage and assembled. Master carpenter John Wilson was left to determine the most efficient means of storage and setup. One season, when five plays were running in the repertory, the actors were required to pass through a narrow tunnel of stored sets in order to get to the stage.

Many of the Asolo's best stagehands were non-theatre people whom Victor Meyrich recruited and trained. A number of them he found in the Idle Hour, a bar on the corner of U.S. 41 and Virginia Drive.

During the rehearsal period, Bert Taylor, the sound technician in those days, had to find the sources for music and sounds that would be recorded and edited for each cue. He made the rounds at record shops, music stores, radio stations and even church choirs.

Catherine "Kit" King, the costume designer, had been with the company since its first summer season in 1960. "We make as many of the costumes as we can for each show," she said; in-house creation was almost mandatory when the play was a period piece. "We try to make the actors look as good as possible, but there's no way to disguise excess weight."

The late Jean Morgan, a loveable curmudgeon known as "Omarr" to her friends, took charge of keeping the costumes clean and in good repair—and sometimes manhandling actors during fast changes. "I treat the actors like I would my kids," she once said. "You temper it with a lot of kindness and a lot of good humor, but you have to use the old iron hand sometimes."

Bob Naismith, the properties master, was responsible for creating the complex devices that must work on stage. While in the navy, Naismith had been a medical technician, assigned to dentistry; so for Asolo productions he could make false teeth for the actors. John Godsey organized the myriad props for each show and would even have to prepare food that was to be eaten on stage. During these first years when there were so many financial and technological limitations, the technical crews relied on ingenuity and hard work to keep the repertory functioning.

During tech week (at that time, the four working days before opening), all the elements were brought together on stage so that the actors could become acclimated to the set, costumes, lights, sound and props. The production was then turned over to my wife, Marian, the production stage manager, who would "call" each performance (a process vaguely like what a quarterback does to coordinate the timing of the other players). At the Asolo, the stage manager was also responsible for scheduling the repertory season, a considerably complicated process of coordinating performances and rehearsals while satisfying Equity rules. (On top of all this, in 1973 Marian had given birth to our twin daughters.) Marty Petlock called the stage manager the "chief, the boss, the captain of the ship, the *capo di tutti capo*. The stage manager's word is backstage law. Once the show is on, no one—not director, producer or featured actor—is above the stage manager."

Marian Wallace, production stage manager, 1968 to 2010. Photo by *Southern Living*.

When all these elements were brought together, the show would open.

The technical precedents Charlie Reimer set during those first years—historical accuracy, craftsmanship, efficiency—evolved into a department that would in time gain national recognition. In 1989, Universal Studios asked the Asolo Scenic Studio to provide the decorative elements for the earthquake attraction at the Orlando theme park. Victor Meyrich and a staff artist put together a portfolio and flew to California. After they made their pitch, the Asolo was awarded the contract. The job lasted for three years and grossed $500,000.

Bob Strane once said, "We have one of the best technical crews in the country. If you want something at this theatre, no matter how unusual or tricky it is, you should ask for it. I never feel that anything is too much to ask in terms of ingenuity."

(As of this writing, the shop has been moved to a new facility with more than thirty-eight thousand square feet of space. At present, the building includes a production area and storage space for props and costumes and will in time include a rehearsal room, educational space and offices. The Robert and Beverly Koski production center was made possible by a very generous donation from Beverly Koski.)

The success of the theatre, the growing support of its regional audience, the innovative repertoire and the recognition by the national press culminated in a significant high point in 1975.

The Public Broadcasting System's *Theater in America* series was producing a 1976 bicentennial season—"a series of theatrical productions by eight of the most outstanding theater companies in the U.S." Jac Venza, executive director of the series, had visited friends in Sarasota and, consequently, became familiar with the Asolo and its success. The Asolo was subsequently chosen as one of the eight companies to produce a play for the bicentennial celebration.

The play, the Asolo's choice, was Sydney Kingsley's *The Patriots*. "Viewers who relished a glimpse of the personalities and conflicts of our Founding Fathers as depicted in *The Adams Chronicle*," said the press release, "will be especially interested in Kingsley's portrayals of three brilliant patriots: Thomas Jefferson, defender of democracy; in constant conflict with Alexander Hamilton, believer in the rule of the rich and powerful elite; with George Washington playing the beloved and respected mediator." The show was to be filmed in Sarasota at the Palm Tree Playhouse, and the cast would be made up primarily of Asolo actors (including Robert Murch as Jefferson, Philip LeStrange as Hamilton and myself as James Madison).

Robert Murch and Ralph Clanton in the Asolo/ Theater in America production of *The Patriots* by Sidney Kingsley. *Photo by Gary W. Sweetman.*

The Patriots went on a brief tour of the state before filming began. Robert Strane directed the stage production; Ken Campbell and Bob Hankel, both of WNET New York, were the producer and director of the televised production, respectively.

Veteran actor Ralph Clanton, whose long résumé included major roles in the film versions of *Othello* and *Cyrano de Bergerac* (both starring Jose Ferrer), was cast as George Washington. Clanton already bore a strong resemblance to the first president, but he was determined to strengthen that resemblance. "I bought some nose putty and practiced with it a bit," he said, "and I had chewing gum inside my lower lip to look like the Gilbert Stuart portrait." The effect was uncanny.

During the tour and after a matinee that had been plagued by mistakes, Bob Strane walked out onto the stage (the house was now empty) in what you could call a high state of dudgeon. He picked up a folding chair and hurled it across the stage. At that moment, Ralph Clanton, still in costume and makeup, appeared from the wings and commanded, "Robert, you stop this! Go home, have a glass of warm milk and go to bed!" They say Bob, very un-Strane-like, sheepishly left the stage. When I asked what had happened, he explained, "I have just been chastised by the father of our country."

The Patriots was broadcast nationally in May and June 1976.

The 1976 season opener, *The New York Idea*, marked the Asolo debut of director John Ulmer. Within twenty years, Ulmer would have earned himself a significant position in the theatre's history.

Howard Millman and Robert Strane in 1976. *Photo by* Southern Living.

Throughout the '70s, one of Dick Fallon's pet projects was the creation of the Charles MacArthur Center for Development of American Theatre—the purpose of which, Dick said, was "to unite professional and educational theatre." Helen Hayes, wife of the late playwright Charles MacArthur, was named honorary chairperson of the board of directors. In November 1974, seed money allowed the center to move forward. "Please God," Miss Hayes implored, "cooperate with Dean Fallon and [FSU president] Dr. Marshall and Charlie up there on cloud nine" to make the MacArthur Center a reality.

In the fall of 1976, the old Palm Tree Playhouse once again became a soundstage, hosting S.N. Behrman's *End of Summer*, the first production of the *American Heritage* television series, which aimed to film the great American classics for educational purposes. Miss Hayes was featured in the role of Mrs. Wyler; she played the part in a wheelchair. I was her butler, Robert, and could later boast that I used to push Helen Hayes around. The Asolo design

Brad Wallace and Helen Hayes during the taping of *End of Summer* by S.N. Berhman. *Photo by Bob Westenhouser.*

and technical staffs were also involved. Ken Campbell and Stephen Porter of WNET New York co-directed.

When Jon Spelman, director of instruction since 1969, left the Asolo in 1974, he took his talents a mere four miles south and founded the Florida Studio Theatre in downtown Sarasota. In its infancy, it was a hand-to-mouth operation, but by the early '80s the theatre had a permanent home, the historic Women's Club on the corner of Palm and Cocoanut Avenues, and was successfully producing new and cutting-edge plays. Jon began a sabbatical in June 1980; former Asolo student Richard Hopkins served as artistic director during Spelman's absence. Richard later took the position full time.

Bob Strane and Howard Millman also recognized the potential in plays that might once have been criticized as controversial. For several seasons, we'd premiered new plays in the repertory—an astonishing practice, as the shows were inserted with very little workshop time and only one preview. Playwrights could stay as long as they liked after the opening and make changes, if they so chose. It was a daring plan that sometimes paid off—as it did in the summer of 1976, when *Win with Wheeler* by Lee Kalcheim premiered at the Asolo. Venerable Broadway producer George Abbot saw the production and picked up the rights. He would direct the play, retitled *Winning Isn't Everything*, at Manhattan's Hudson Guild Theatre in 1978.

After the success of the late '70s, Bob Strane felt he could be more adventurous with his choices in the future. "A few years ago," he said, "they wanted light comedies, but now they're asking for more 'Shadow Boxes.'" (*The Shadow Box* was a play that dealt with death from the vantage point of residents of a California hospice.) "I think audiences are realizing you can't run away from contemporary problems."

It was in 1980 that the Asolo once again divided its season into three parts. From February through April there would be three plays presented in rotating repertory, then a month-long straight-run of a musical or musical revue (with a separate company) and then a summer repertory season of three plays.

The "Soaring '70s" became a high-water mark for the Asolo. The theatre received a number of grants, co-producers began to contribute substantially to individual productions, the Asolo Angels continued to increase their fundraising and the support of the regional business community continued to grow. A poll showed that 82 percent of out-of-town theatregoers listed the Asolo as one of the principal reasons for visiting Sarasota, and 67 percent of new residents gave the theatre as their main reason for moving to Sarasota. The Asolo was now sponsored by the Festival Association, the State of Florida, Florida State University and the Ringling Museum.

During the '70s, season box office sales averaged over 90 percent of capacity (98 percent in 1976 and 1977). If houses were consistently full, consensus determined that the next logical step was to build a somewhat larger theatre with "the charm of the smaller one," said Howard Millman. "It's going to be very hard to do, but I think it may become a necessity."

Chapter 7

Major Changes

I don't see how you can congratulate yourself for an adventurous play choice when there's no audience to support it.
—Bob Strane

In April 1980, Howard Millman announced that on July 1 he would resign as managing director to become executive director of the Pittsburgh Public Theater. "Howard Millman has provided magnificent leadership as managing director," said Dick Fallon. "Through his efforts, the Asolo has grown to capacity audiences and gained a national reputation. I shall miss him as a dear friend and a respected, valued colleague, and I wish him every success and happiness in his new position."

Howard was effusive in his thanks to the many supporters who had kept the Asolo alive, but he warned that the community should not become complacent about supporting an institution that had had such impact on the west coast of Florida's cultural and economic life. He wanted to convince the business community that additional support was essential: "We need a new building that would hold at least 600 people," he said. "Without a new theatre, ticket prices will have to be increased so dramatically in years to come that a large part of the community will be priced out of the picture." David Levenson, who had served on the administrative staff of the Cleveland Symphony, became the Asolo's new managing director.

A year later, artistic director Bob Strane announced that he, too, was resigning his position and would be leaving Sarasota in the summer of 1981. He had, as noted in the *Sarasota Herald-Tribune*, guided the Asolo's growth "from a summer theater with an $8,000 budget to a million dollar operation with a nationwide reputation for excellence, [and] he was moving on." His announcement was a surprise to Asolo supporters and a special blow to those of us in the company who'd known him for so many years.

"I worry that the person who follows me may not be fighter enough," he said. "The fight to get quality is what makes the job of an artistic director so difficult. You have to be continually alert in order to do better all the time. You can't ride on your success, and you can't depend on the goodwill of others. The threats you face can come from within the organization or without, and inertia is one of your biggest enemies."

Bob saw the Asolo Theatre as "unique and gorgeous," but, like Howard Millman, he insisted upon his departure that the company needed a much bigger space if it was to survive, as was reported in this piece from the *Sarasota Herald-Tribune* in 1981:

> [The original theatre] *simply seats too few people to justify the cost of running it. I hope the present theatre could be retained for intimate productions that work best there. Another bigger theatre could be used for the "biggies."*
>
> *I don't want the Asolo to become an elitist toy, the darling of some set. And I don't think the people who might be described as within that set would want it either. They don't want this theatre to become an exclusive club. The Asolo needs a broad base, and its goal must be to find a new avenue of access.*
>
> *If I were to start all over, I would start at a much earlier point trying to develop playwrights, develop new works, and to use more of the resources of this theatre to do that than we have done.*
>
> *In addition to being an idealist and a fanatic and crazy and various other things, I'm also very practical. And I don't think theatre occurs when there's no exchange, no flow of energy across the footlights. I don't see how you can congratulate yourself for an adventurous play choice when there's no audience for it.*
>
> *Our community support is a class act. There is an emotional bond that supporters have that goes beyond bucks. People don't just support this theatre, they love it.*

English director Peter Brook had once posed the question regarding the theatre: "Who needs it? Why should anyone take the trouble to see it?"

"That's a good question," was Bob's take on the matter. "You better know the answer. Even if you're not able to explain it, you better know it." Soon after leaving Sarasota, Bob became the director of dramatic studies at the Houston Grand Opera Conservatory.

Stuart Vaughn became the Asolo's artistic advisor as a temporary replacement. He'd been a major artistic force behind the formation of the New York Shakespeare Festival and the revival of New York's Phoenix Theatre. His New York directing credits included *Richard III* with a young George C. Scott in the title role, *The Taming of the Shrew* with Colleen Dewhurst and *Abe Lincoln in Illinois* with Hal Holbrook. Stuart was responsible for choosing the plays, actors and designers for the '82 season. Some of the plays he chose to produce were *The Male Animal*, *Charley's Aunt* and *Mrs. Warren's Profession*.

When asked about doing new plays, he said, "I don't believe in announcing 'A new American Play' and then trying to find one, because you might have to settle for something second rate. I do think that the function of such a [regional] theatre is to do classics of the recent and distant past as well as brand-new plays."

While making a speech in Titusville, Florida, in November 1981, Dick Fallon collapsed and was subsequently hospitalized for several days. The doctors diagnosed exhaustion and advised he slow down. 'Twas not exactly the Fallon style.

He retired as dean of the School of Theatre in 1982 and was then named dean emeritus and director of professional programs at FSU. In August, he became president of the American Theatre Association; in September, he was named one of FSU's Burt Reynolds Professors of Professional and Regional Theatre and would also occupy FSU's Eminent Scholar's Chair. His responsibilities also included supervision of the Asolo, the State Theatre Board, Players State Theatre in Miami (made a state theatre in 1977), the Burt Reynolds actor training program in Jupiter and the Tallahassee-based MacArthur Center. "They say I am trying to build an empire," he said. "But if Fallon is the glue that holds it together, then I have done a terrible disservice. I would like to be able to pass this on."

Gil Lazier, a teacher, actor and director with an impressive résumé who had joined the FSU faculty in 1970, took Fallon's place as dean of the School of Theatre. Gil had been president of the Association for Theatre in Higher Education, commissioner for the National Association of Schools of Theatre and vice-president of the International Theatre Institute/U.S. His honors included a life membership in the College of Fellows of the American Theatre and the National Theater Conference and a Career Achievement Award from the Florida Theater Conference.

Gil had been teaching at Columbia University in New York City when Dick Fallon, an old acquaintance, invited him to lunch at the Lamb's Club. It was Dick's hope to persuade him to come to FSU and take over the theatre's graduate program. Gil, a fan of the Asolo's productions, had been intrigued by the possibility of developing a graduate program during its efforts to expand.

Within a year, a permanent replacement for Bob Strane was found. John Ulmer had successfully directed *The New York Idea*, *Design for Living* and *Cyrano de Bergerac* for the Asolo in the '70s; the Sarasota audience already knew him well. John had been artistic director at Stage West in Springfield, Massachusetts, and was the founding artistic director of the Carnegie-Mellon Theater Company. He assumed the artistic director position on August 1, 1982.

John Ulmer was not reticent about his plans for the Asolo's future. Come his second season, he said, he would scrap both the rotating repertory and the resident company. "Repertory has been a tradition around here, and like most traditions it has attained an importance that perhaps it doesn't

John Ulmer.

really deserve." Dropping the repertory would also make the company more attractive to New York–based actors ("bigger talents," as he described them), who could be lured to Florida for a single production but might be reluctant to invest a full season away from the city. He felt that people got all "misty-eyed" about repertory and the versatility of the actors but that doing more than one play at a time tended to disrupt the actors' concentration, and therefore there was always a good chance the product would be slapdash. "Repertory always smacks of a fast food chain," he said, "and that worries me."

Instead, John focused on new plays. "If you hit the jackpot with one and your theatre goes to New York, it brings distinction to the area as well as money in the form of grants and so forth." But he felt limited because of the facility he had inherited. "We should be into the nuclear thing and abortion. We should be the center of what's going on. The problem is, with that darned theatre, people think they're going to a museum."

John's plan was to begin his second season with a combination of straight-run shows and possibly a two-show repertory, with separate casts. Other changes: the Asolo would begin its '83–84 season in December and close in July instead of early September; the theatre would try to hire established Broadway stars for some shows (George C. Scott and Maureen Stapleton had been mentioned); and there would be an effort to produce new plays.

Bette Oliver died on her day off in May 1983 after the closing of Shaw's *Misalliance*, in which she played Mrs. Tarleton. She was an enormous talent and had been one of the Asolo's most popular actresses. The performance space in the Frankel Building became the Bette Oliver Theatre.

Chapter 8

A Bold New Plan

I'm in a position to be of help. Use me.
—Burt Reynolds

Burton L. Reynolds enrolled at FSU in 1954 on a football scholarship, showing great promise as a freshman running back on the Seminole team that went to the Sun Bowl that year. But his aspirations for a professional football career were shattered when he seriously injured his knee in a car accident. He returned to his home in South Florida and enrolled in Palm Beach Junior College, where he soon discovered the theatre and acting. He won the college's annual drama award and was subsequently spotted by the sister of a Hollywood producer who arranged for a screen test. In 1959, the up-and-coming young actor sent a letter to FSU's alumni affairs director. "I hope to return to FSU someday," he said. "If you should ever, for some cockeyed reason, want anything from me, please feel free to ask."

Back in 1979, Reynolds had approached Dick Fallon and outlined his plans to start an actor-training program at his dinner theatre, the Burt Reynolds Institute for Theatre, in Jupiter, Florida. "The 'Bandit' and I are men of one mind," Dick said. "We dislike academic stuffiness and believe that contact with the professional 'real world' is the only way for young people to learn the essentials of a performance career." Dick eagerly welcomed the Burt Reynolds Institute for Theatre into the FSU fold. "If a young person comes to me and says 'I want to become a movie star,'" he later said, "I'll tell him to go with Reynolds. He'll tell you how." In September 1980, Reynolds made it possible for FSU to fund a million-dollar endowed chair under the Eminent Scholar's Program. When he received his honorary doctorate at

FSU in 1982, he said, "I will love this university for the rest of my life, and I will try to make you proud of me."

Meanwhile, just before Christmas 1983, rumors circulated that Sarasota could become home to a multimillion-dollar complex that would produce theatre, television and film. The community buzzed about the prospect of national recognition. The *Sarasota Herald-Tribune* reported:

> *For years, Asolo State Theatre officials have expressed their need for a new and much larger theater facility. On Thursday, they'll ask the Ringling Museum Board of Trustees to provide the land for the project. The board will be asked to consider leasing the Asolo a parcel of museum-owned land between U.S. 41 and Bayshore Road. The lease proposal also covers the 18th century Baroque interior of the present Asolo building, which would be incorporated into the new facility.* [Something in the range of seven hundred seats was suggested for the mainstage.] *Actor Burt Reynolds is the major force behind the project, which already has received financial commitment from the Florida legislature. The complex would include one and possibly two theater buildings, as well as facilities for video-taping, film production and post production work. Prominent New York and Hollywood actors are expected to become involved in the project.*

Richard Carroll, the museum's director, said he thought the museum would support the project but would need building plans before going forward. The fire had been kindled.

Governor Bob Graham and members of the state legislature loved the idea of making Florida more attractive to the television and film industry. They appropriated $575,000 for a feasibility study of Reynolds's project, which had become known as "The Theatre Inc." Though the details changed throughout its development, its main component was to be a nine-hundred-seat theatre in which productions featuring star performers could be filmed and distributed. The ultimate goal would be to establish a production center to rival southern California and New York.

Dick Fallon laid out the major points regarding the Asolo's involvement in the new venture in a statement released on January 5, 1984.

One, the Asolo company and the original theatre would be included in the new complex, and both theatres would operate under one umbrella management. Using parts now in storage, the original theatre would be expanded to 450 to 500 seats, and the existing building now housing the theatre would be used for administrative purposes by the museum and as a lecture hall.

(But, portentously, there were in fact no extra parts in storage: Bob Strane had directed John Gay's *The Beggar's Opera* for the 1980–81 season. The set was designed to create a mirror image of the Asolo, so that whether seated in the auditorium or seated on the stage, the image before you would be the same: royal box facing royal box. For reasons unknown, the set was dismantled and stored in the museum. This mistakenly led to the notion that there were extra parts that could be used to expand the theatre.)

Two, the artistic and technical staffs would be interchangeable. Income from television programs would benefit both theatres, and the present conservatory would be a preparatory step toward more advanced training in dramatic arts. That training would involve practical experience under the finest professional craftsmen and artists in television and theatre production. A national cable or television program might be produced on a regular basis featuring work done at The Theatre Inc. and Reynolds's dinner theatre in Jupiter, Florida.

And three, when all was incorporated, Sarasota would be home to the Asolo, The Theatre Inc., Fallon's and Hayes' MacArthur Center and the Frankel Building.

On February 6, 1984, Burt Reynolds, speaking from the Asolo stage, outlined his plans for The Theatre Inc. It would, he said, "make Sarasota a national center for live theatre, television and film." The planned nine-hundred-seat mainstage theatre would be flanked by a large video studio and would "become the country's only theatre specifically designed to videotape, film or broadcast performances as they happen before audiences." The design would be such that neither actors nor audience would ever see a camera.

But there was one small problem: at least two other Florida cities were in the running for the project. Sarasota supporters helped the cause by agreeing to pay half the cost of the new center. No other city came up with a comparable offer.

By mid-February, it became official: Sarasota had indeed been chosen as the home for The Theatre Inc. In reaching his decision, Reynolds said, "I've rarely met with such organized, enthusiastic support in any community—running the gamut from political to business to civic and social leaders—and I am terribly excited about working with them all to bring our dream for The Theatre to a reality." He would contribute $1 million to the project, and his generosity wouldn't stop there. When Dick Fallon, Governor Bob Graham and a group of legislators traveled to Virginia to meet with Reynolds (where he was filming *Best Friends*), he said to them, "Look, I'm No. 1 at the box office, but it won't last long. Now I'm in a position to be of help. Use me."

Richard Fallon as Willie Loman in *Death of a Salesman* by Arthur Miller. *Photo by Gary W. Sweetman.*

Said Dick Fallon, "[It was] a dream of mine that there not only be a marriage between the academic and professional theatre, but a marriage between the regional, not-for-profit theatre and commercial sector."

In April 1984, the Asolo celebrated its twenty-fifth anniversary with a production of Arthur Miller's *Death of a Salesman*. To fill his spare time, Dick Fallon played the part of Willie Loman.

There were some hard feelings in other parts of the state when it was announced that Sarasota had won the prize. Palm Beach let it be known that they were prepared to make a counteroffer if plans could not be consummated. The *Miami Herald*'s Bill Cosford wrote that The Theatre Inc. would be a "boondoggle" if constructed in Sarasota. Miami, he said, was already the center of the state's film and video industry. Sarasota's state congressman, Robert Johnson, responded that Cosford "sounds like a jealous suitor watching someone else walk down the aisle."

The Theatre Inc. complex would be built in Sarasota, but where? The first choice was to stay within the confines of the museum. According to Edie Anson, a spokesperson for the Asolo, a ten-acre site would have to be donated before the project could move forward. At this time, however, the Ringling Museum had not officially offered land, and according to Mark Gotlob, the museum's associate director for administration, "Looking at an aerial map, I don't really see any 10-acre plots that are open." Other possibilities included land on the east side of U.S. 41 that was owned by the Sarasota-Bradenton Airport, another spot near New College and a location on DeSoto Road. Added to the mix were the concerns of John Ringling's descendents, who feared The Theatre Inc. might tarnish the museum's image as the world's premier collection of Baroque art. The Ringling Museum's board of directors adopted those concerns and delayed permission to use museum property for the complex.

John Ulmer had written a supportive letter to the editor during this time, saying, "I have considerable experience to buttress my belief that a merger of the Asolo and The Theatre Inc., is the best opportunity the Asolo may ever have to fulfill its purpose grandly. People who think the Asolo should only do Restoration comedies or something on the level of *I Love Lucy* re-runs had better not come this year." (At this point, the Asolo's last Baroque period play had been produced three years before.) Like John Ulmer, the *Clearwater Sun* argued in support of Reynolds's vision: "While most dinner theatres cater to audiences and serve up their favorites—however hackneyed—Reynolds's theatre does not. By selling subscriptions, like a legitimate theatre, it can offer more adventurous works."

In the midst of these changes, managing director David Levenson left the Asolo to become the executive director of the New Orleans Philharmonic Orchestra. One writer observed, "An era is ending at the Asolo Theatre and David S. Levenson decided to go with it."

In his parting comments, David bemoaned the original theatre's 312-seat size: "For a hit at the Asolo, we can turn away 100 people a night—as much as $1,000 a night. It doesn't take long for that to add up to $30,000 or $40,000."

The 1984–85 season would include a couple of old chestnuts (*The Little Foxes* and *You Can't Take It with You*) but was largely made up of contemporary plays. *Children of a Lesser God*, *Amadeus*, *Night, Mother* and *Sister Mary Ignatius Explains It All for You* had all been recent New York successes. (The latter, however, would never be produced at the Asolo; some suggest the Catholic Legion of Decency may have scared the Asolo board into recanting.) There were many, however, who were disappointed that for the third year in a row, the season would not include a play by Shakespeare. John Ulmer responded,

"We've got to reach a broader audience. This is not an elitist theatre and we can't have people thinking that the Asolo is not a place to have fun." The actors were also disappointed we weren't doing Shakespeare.

Other plays produced during John Ulmer's tenure spanned an eclectic range, from lighter fare to Greek classics: *The Dining Room*, *A View from the Bridge*, *The Gin Game*, *Waiting for Godot*, *Dames at Sea*, *How the Other Half Loves*, *A Moon for the Misbegotten*, *Orphans*, *As You Like It*, *Pump Boys and Dinettes*, *Frankie and Johnny in the Claire de Lune* and *Medea.*

There were some concerns that plans for The Theatre Inc. were moving too slowly and that a lack of PR could cause the public to lose interest. "We would not go so far as to say that the project has been stalled," read one editorial in the *Sarasota Herald-Tribune*, "but it has been moving with less speed than deliberation." The same article also urged, "Anything that is done to help The Theatre must also help the John and Mable Ringling Museum, the Asolo Theatre, the State of Florida and the Sarasota-Manatee community." Lastly, it referenced a rumor that Burt Reynolds was not in the best of health and that this might affect his enthusiasm for the new venture.

During the summer of 1984, the *Los Angeles Times* published an article by Charles Champlin headed "Burt Reynolds shifting to the slow lane." For three months Reynolds had suffered from the effects of kidney stones and an inner-ear infection that had affected his balance. He admitted that these ailments exaggerated the toll of a very strenuous career in filmmaking, and so he had decided not to act in movies for at least a year. But even as the kidney stones became fodder for the tabloids, he managed to keep his good humor. "I would be waiting in terrible pain," he said, "and the television would be reporting, 'It's in the urinary tract but should appear at any moment.' I asked myself, would Cary Grant be standing there with a tea strainer, waiting? When I write my story, I'll call it 'Ejecting the Stone.'"

In October 1985, the Ringling Trustees approved a plan that would give The Theatre Inc. property on the Ringling grounds northeast of the museum. However, the trustees' resolution did not include moving the Asolo's ornate interior into the new complex. Instead, The Theatre Inc. would build an entirely new home for the Asolo company. "It's unthinkable to have the Asolo without its 18th-century interior," the *Bradenton Herald* responded. "Worse, TWO Asolos—one the theater company that performs plays and the other the 18th-century interior that sits as a museum piece. Surely no one who supported the Reynolds's project dreamed that it could mean separating the theater company from its Renaissance setting."

Fortunately, there were caveats. Museum spokesmen said that only a master plan had been approved, and moving the Asolo interior was merely one of the loose ends yet to be resolved. Meanwhile, a search was underway for an architect to design a structure for the two theatres. The Asolo company could be performing in its new home by the 1986–87 season.

Steve Rothman became Dick Fallon's associate executive director in December 1985. Steve grew up in Sarasota and developed his passion for the theatre by attending performances at the Asolo. He had spent time as an adolescent student actor and had later been an Asolo apprentice actor while majoring in theatre at FSU (he also received his master's degree there). He'd been Howard Millman's graduate assistant during the 1973–74 season.

Steve Rothman built an impressive résumé that positioned him perfectly for the new developments in Sarasota: he'd worked in audience development at the Hartman Theatre Company and served as producing director of the Paramount Arts Theatre in Chicago. In 1979, Steve moved to California to oversee the renovation of the Pasadena Playhouse, where stars like Robert Young, William Holden and Gene Hackman had received their early training. (He'd been able to enlist these stars and many more to support the drive to restore the playhouse.) Television actress Sally Struthers said of Steve, "He's armed with exuberance, talent and an inordinate amount of daring." His friend Ed Asner once called him "the best kind of conman—sincere."

Some Asolo supporters feared the company would become a "poor stepchild" to a complex built around a nine-hundred-seat house featuring star performers. Steve attempted to allay these fears. "The Asolo has been a part of my life since I was a kid," he said. "I'd never go along with anything that would damage it." He wanted the Asolo "to rejuvenate itself, to reach the level of national prominence that it richly deserves." In turn, The Theatre Inc. would benefit by its association with an established institution that already operated the kind of actor training program Reynolds had envisioned from the beginning.

In February 1985, secretary of state George Firestone spoke to a group of business and government leaders and told them that the arts provided one of the best returns on their investment. "The corporate community has not been putting back—in terms of arts and culture—anywhere near what they're taking out," he said. "Total support for the arts from the corporate community in Florida probably doesn't even reach 7 percent." The state of Florida was to set an example. Less than three months later, Governor Bob Graham presented a check for $4 million to Dick Fallon for The Theatre Inc. project.

Local publication *Our Town Sarasota* suggested another purpose for The Theatre Inc. "By videotaping the recollections of renowned performers while they are appearing as part of Theatre Inc. productions, the center will accumulate an unheralded collection of information about individual personalities and general movements in the theatrical and performing arts arena."

But would this kind of project be able to attract nationally known actors and directors? Steve Rothman and Dick Fallon took the first steps in demonstrating that this was feasible.

On a Saturday in early June, a mélange of stars who would have been known to most of the western world at that time were assembled at the Asolo to show their support for The Theatre Inc. project. The guests included Dana Andrews, Isabel Sanford, Henry Polic II, William Windom, Dianne Ladd, Laura Durnn, Bob Denver and Alan Arkin. Burt Reynolds couldn't be there but was represented by his personal manager, David Gershenson.

Steve stressed that those stars in attendance were willing to come back to work at The Theatre Inc. He also said that others—including Karl Malden, José Ferrer, Martin Landau, Harry Morgan, Eli Wallach and Anne Jackson—had expressed a "keen interest" in the project.

"The point of the event," wrote Kevin Dean in the *Longboat Observer*, "was to dramatize through the media the support among the national acting community for this unprecedented center for the performing arts and to kick off the local fundraising drive." Of the $3.5 million needed from the Sarasota area, more than $500,000 had been raised.

Elizabeth Lindsay, a major fundraiser for the project, was asked if she anticipated problems getting the community to produce all of the money that had been pledged. "I don't think so," she said. "When you're talking about raising this much money, it takes time." Elizabeth also announced that the celebrities would be meeting with local and state politicians and business leaders. And what those celebrities had to say was very supportive:

Alan Arkin:

> *We are not just "playing Hollywood." The theatre can change lives. The theatre isn't just a glamour industry or a way to pass the time. It can rip someone out of this small vision of themselves.*

Isabel Sanford:

> *I have worked in a great many regional companies. We need this thing all over the country, especially now.*

Bob Denver:

> *I think that once this is finished every state in the union will want a place like this.*

Milton Goldman (the agent who helped form the careers of Sir Laurence Olivier, Sir John Gielgud, Albert Finney, Meryl Streep and Lee Marvin):

> *Theatre in this country is in a really desperate state. Regional theatres like this develop the stars of tomorrow. They allow actors to test their strengths and weaknesses. On Broadway you don't get a chance to fail.*

Dick Fallon predicted the groundbreaking would take place by the end of the year (1985) and that the structure would be completed by the end of 1986.

But problems persisted. "For public consumption," wrote the *Sarasota Herald-Tribune*, "both the board and The Theatre Inc. are expressing positive assurance that the $10 million complex will be built on museum ground… There are mutterings, though, that such a scenario may not be the final one." Also, "grave questions" persisted as to whether the allocated space could provide parking for both the theatre and a new visitors' center the museum planned to build.

The museum board conceded the necessary acreage in October, and the Asolo was given permission to build the new complex on museum property. But despite the community's great disappointment, the original Asolo would not be moved. Instead, a modern four-hundred-seat theatre in a separate building adjacent to the nine-hundred-seat mainstage would become the Asolo company's new home.

In September, Gulf Coast Constructors signed a construction management contract with the Asolo board of directors. The Asolo construction committee, a subcommittee of the board, then chose two consultants to work with Gulf Coast: Theatre Projects Consultants Ltd., which was based in London, and Stuart Barger, a highly regarded Sarasota architect.

Theatre Projects had an international reputation and had been involved in the design of London's National Theatre, the Barbizion Center (the home of the Royal Shakespeare Company) and the Vivian Beaumont in New York's Lincoln Center. Stuart Barger, who had worked with Gulf Coast before, was to play a major role in more than one aspect of the Asolo's future. Victor Meyrich (by then the Asolo's technical director, and eventually the Asolo's production manager) regarded him as "the smartest guy I've ever met."

Richard Pilbrow, the head of Theatre Projects, expected the nine-hundred-seat theatre to have at least two levels. He said:

> *Our goal is to make it as efficient a machine as any television studio and yet not have the audience aware of the videotaping aspects. The thing that excites me about this project is the extraordinary number of dedicated people involved. Frequently, one gets involved with projects in which the owners are constructing a building but they don't really know what they want to put in it. Here, you already have such impressive work, such enormous productivity, coming out of the existing Asolo.*

In the Decembers of '85 and '86, the Asolo did an adaptation of Dickens's *A Christmas Carol.* It was a family affair both years: I played Bob Cratchit, Marian stage managed and our three daughters also played characters in the production. For a month of rehearsals and another of performances, the five of us could drive to and from the theatre together.

Bettilu Lewis died in early April 1986. With Chick Frankel, she had been a vital part of the Asolo's growth in the '60s and '70s. During her time as executive director of the Asolo Angels, membership rose from seven hundred to four thousand.

Chapter 9

Out with the Old

The Lengthened shadow of the man
—Sarasota Herald-Tribune

Between mid-April and mid-November 1986, the Asolo underwent changes that radically redirected its future.

Rumors had been circulating, and in April the *Sarasota Herald-Tribune* reported that the boards of the Asolo and The Theatre Inc. were about to merge as the "Asolo Performing Arts Center." A committee had already been appointed to search for an executive director for the new operation. Supporters wondered why Asolo's longtime leader, Dick Fallon, was being asked to step down. Board members Elizabeth Lindsay, Jim Scheurenbrand and Robert Wilhelm tried to justify the need for new leadership. "We're at the stage of this project where we need to look nationally for the best administrative director to run the entire operation," said Wilhelm. Florida State University president Bernard Sliger, also a board member, argued, "I see the need for strong administrative leadership, and feel we must now seek a new chief executive officer for this multimillion-dollar project."

The board gave other reasons, too. Dick, whose responsibilities included being executive director of both the Asolo and The Theatre Inc., as well as heading the acting program at the Burt Reynolds Institute in Jupiter, would not have the time to devote all his energy to a project as big and complex as The Theatre. Impatient board members fretted over a perceived lack of substantive progress, and others said privately that Dick was an ineffective leader whose style inhibited fundraising. Also, Dick, who was sixty-two at the time, had recently undergone quadruple bypass surgery.

"We're certainly not trying to freeze Dick out," continued board member Wilhelm. "He would still play a major role. We still need his input on the artistic end of things. It's not a war. It's not a case of us against Dick." The Theatre Inc.'s new board chairman, Jim Scheurenbrand, assured, "Everyone involved in this project has the same motivation: To produce this dream of Fallon's and Reynold's."

"I conceived this project," Dick fired back in a newspaper interview, "and I will remain its executive director." He insisted he would only relinquish control when the new theatre was functioning and the leadership could be turned over to someone who shared his dream. "The project isn't about creating a building; it's the artistic product that will make the theatre come alive. You can't just bring someone in from the outside to administer a complex if you don't have a clear idea of what's going to take place on the inside. If that happens, you'll have a white elephant here—a theatre that's nothing more than an empty shell."

Tension increased. Dick was the one who'd originally appointed Lindsay, Wilhelm and Scheurenbrand to the board. "Like Dr. Frankenstein," he said, "I may have created a monster." (Though he later apologized for the remark: "I'm sorry if I implied that anyone involved has anything but the best interests of the Asolo and The Theatre Inc. program at heart," he said. "I want to do everything I can to reduce the tension and get beyond the personalities. The Asolo and The Theatre Inc. mean everything to me, and I don't want to do anything that might jeopardize what we've accomplished.")

Many Asolo supporters believed Dick was being made a scapegoat by the board; Asolo actors and staff were in disbelief. We alternately commiserated and gnashed our teeth backstage and at dinner parties. In April, when Dick called a meeting of the company in the Frankel Building and told us that he had no intention of stepping down, he received a standing ovation. People organized petitions on his behalf. Still, Dick remained diplomatic: "Divisions like that won't do anybody any good."

In mid-April, just weeks after he was first asked to step down, Dick was dealt yet another blow. Steve Rothman, Dick's handpicked heir apparent, announced that he was leaving the Asolo. Steve insisted that his decision had nothing to do with the current problems but was rather a personal matter. (His fiancée, Alma Martinez, was a film and stage actress in Los Angeles, and the cross-country separation was putting a strain on their relationship.) "For the first time," he said, "I'm putting my personal life ahead of my career."

But Steve later revealed that Scheurenbrand had asked him months earlier if he would be interested in a leadership role. "I told him, if Dick wanted to step down for some reason, I'd be interested," he responded. "But I wouldn't accept it under any other circumstances." Dick, he now knew, was not willing to step down.

Dick's control of The Theatre's future continued to wane. Florida State University requested that he spend his time between Tallahassee and Burt Reynolds's actors' training program in Jupiter. Dick conceded that he had expressed interest in returning to Tallahassee but reiterated that he wanted to wait for a successor who shared his vision. (He suggested Don Schoenbaum, a Sarasota resident who had once been managing director of the Guthrie Theater in Minneapolis.)

"Nobody's out to get Dick or anyone else," insisted William Strode, chairman of the Asolo board. "There's no conspiracy here. Anything we've done is in response to FSU's plans." With Steve Rothman gone, Dick Fallon admitted that he could not continue to be responsible for programs in Tallahassee, Jupiter and Sarasota simultaneously. If there was to be a change, he wanted to avoid a "jagged transition." He took some solace in the prospect of being an important advisor, saying he'd "gotten assurance that I will have—in fact, I must have—final say in who will be the executive there."

Jim Schuerenbrand told the *Tampa Tribune* that while the board would solicit Dick's recommendations, he would not have the final say.

On May 20, 1986, Dick Fallon's formal resignation was announced. Response from old friends and the community gave testament to his enormous contributions:

Isa Thomas (long a popular and prominent Asolo actress):

> *Why anyone else should come in to finish Dick's creation when he's here to do it is beyond me. None of us would be here without Dick Fallon. I don't think any of them* [The Theatre Inc. board members] *have even been to the theatre.*

Steve Rothman:

> *Dick is the greatest visionary I've ever met in the theatre. To separate him from this project would be like separating a father from his family. I feel strongly that he should remain executive director. As long as he has an associate to help him, I see no reason why he can't administer Theatre Inc. and Jupiter.*

John Ulmer:

> *I'm deeply sorry that it turned out this way. I owe the man a great deal. I like him. He believed in what I did. Most arts organizations are run by despots. What Dick gives the people he employs is freedom. Freedom for creative people. That is an extremely rare thing.*

From an editorial in the *Sarasota Herald-Tribune*:

> *Fallon's resignation doesn't obscure the reality that Asolo is another example of the institution being the lengthened shadow of the man. It was he who created the state theatre, and his work and reason not only provided continuing live theatre to this area, but with its traveling troupes it helped to educate the youngsters of the state to the delights of that form of entertainment—something many of them would not have otherwise known. We hope that the association of the man and theatre, man and community is not ending.*

It had become too much, Dick admitted—the responsibility to FSU, Jupiter and the Asolo. "I had intended," he said, "to see the plan through to its fruition…But to protect all three projects, I'm doing what I hope will serve the best interests of all."

And so he left the Asolo, my old friend and mentor. In retrospect, there may have been mistakes, but there can be no doubt that Dick Fallon dedicated himself, heart and soul, to the cultural growth of the region and the state. He was the Asolo's cornerstone, and without his vision and leadership the Asolo Theatre Festival could not have survived past the '60s.

An acquaintance once said of Dick Fallon that he was the greatest visionary she had ever known—which was, I believe, a succinct description. He was tireless in his quest to bring professional standards to theatre education. Above all, he was one of the world's nicest and most generous people.

Controversy regarding the overall concept of The Theatre Inc. grew, and in June 1986 another change dramatically altered what had been envisioned years before by Dick Fallon and Burt Reynolds. The Theatre Inc. would no longer be used to film productions. People like Elizabeth Lindsay supported the change. It would have been an "interesting experiment," she said, but modern technology was making such an approach obsolete. She felt combining television and live performances was not feasible; that it was a "match between a donkey and a thoroughbred." Besides, it might be difficult to bring the Asolo audience from the historic theatre into such a modern ambience.

The sequence of events was best related by Charlie Husking in the *Sarasota Herald-Tribune* on June 10, 1986:

> *Theatre Inc. is on a new course that will emphasize film, television and theatrical training instead of the videotaping of live performances by featuring well-known actors as planned. The controversy surrounding the project all but evaporated Monday at a Sarasota meeting involving Theatre Inc. board members, state officials and the film industry experts who had criticized the original concept. All parties pledged to cooperate in building an educational training program that will be unique in Florida. Although no votes were taken, it is clear that the complex will no longer include a 900-seat theater designed with videotaping capabilities. Instead, space will be used for a film and television studio, post-production facilities and classrooms. The complex still will include a 400-seat theater that will be the new home of the Asolo State Theatre company. Members of the Florida Motion Picture, Television and Recording Industry Advisory Council have said that* [video taping] *is a faulty premise because the cable television market has dried up. Council members also have criticized The Theatre Inc. design plans, saying the studio space was inadequate to operate a viable training program. "We had a program, and now it has to be rewritten," said board member Bob Wilhelm. "The cable market isn't what we were told it would be. We have accepted 100 percent that there has to be a change in direction." Theatre Inc. chairman Jim Scheurenbrand said, "We are starting from a blank sheet of paper as far as the functional design goes… The training program, which will likely involve 50 film, television and theater students, will be administered by Florida State University." Milt Felsen, a council member and a Sarasota resident, also has been elected to the board. Felsen called the complex "a feather in Sarasota's cap and a project that will benefit all of the dramatic arts."*

After Dick Fallon's resignation, The Theatre Inc. began to be absorbed by the Asolo Center, and after a time, its name faded away entirely.

Chapter 10

In with the New

Our first priority was to find someone with excellent administrative skills…who would be able to work with the politicians in Tallahassee.
—Charles Murphy

Though The Theatre Inc. was fading, legislators were still enamored with the idea of growing Florida's film industry. The state offered $450,000 from the governor's discretionary fund if the Asolo established a film conservatory. A soundstage and other necessary space would have to be part of the program statement.

Uncertainty hovered around what film and television degrees would be offered in the new conservatory. The first plan outlined a two-year master's program: a student's first year would be spent in Tallahassee studying the basics of film and the second in Sarasota, where the new facility would prepare students to become production managers, producers, directors, cinematographers, writers and post-production employees such as editors and soundtrack specialists.

Don Ungurait was a member of the Motion Picture Advisory Council and an associate professor at FSU. He described filmmaking in Florida as a "cottage industry" (Florida was then a distant third behind California and New York), but Ungurait believed a graduate program could change that. "A conservatory at Asolo could produce a new generation of independent Florida filmmakers—not necessarily allied to New York or California—and not a group of transients," he said. "We're talking about building a new Hollywood."

The newly formed Asolo Performing Arts Center was to have submitted plans for the new complex by July. But when the Ringling Museum trustees met, they realized there still were no plans to consider; another extension would be necessary. The new deadline was set for October 13, 1986.

"Sarasota is expected to become a hub for Florida's booming motion picture industry when the state's first school opens in the Asolo Performing Arts Center next year," said Ungurait, who had become the acting director of FSU's film program. The twenty-four students admitted might not have undergraduate degrees in filmmaking but would be "dynamic people who will be catalytic converters for one another…Within ten years, the conservatory will be recognized as one of the nation's premiere film schools in a league with those of the University of Southern California and New York University."

Ungurait spoke of a "Creative Crescent" of production stretching from Orlando west along I-4 and south along I-75 to Sarasota. Disney officials agreed to let conservatory students use their studios for production work.

Stuart Kaminsky, who had been the chairman of Northwestern University's film department, would be director of the new film and TV conservatory. He was an accomplished writer of novels, textbooks, biographies and screenplays (the latter including Sergio Leone's *Once Upon a Time In America*). He had earned a PhD in filmmaking at Northwestern, where he taught for seventeen years. Stuart believed his students should have a strong academic background but that the program should be "specifically designed and equipped to prepare the students for jobs in the film and television industry." The resident faculty of four would be supplemented with guest instructors.

In mid-August '86, Donald P. Creason was appointed the Asolo's new chief spokesman and interim administrative head. Don Creason was associate dean for administrative affairs at FSU's School of Theatre, had extensive experience as a set and lighting designer and had produced more than forty-seven plays. He was known as a "practical administrator," an attribute obviously essential to an endeavor that had lost its way. Dick Fallon, a close friend, supported Don, who insisted that the building project would go forward, though he recognized that major changes had to be made. A larger theatre for the Asolo company was a top priority in order to keep ticket prices from going up, and everyone agreed that a "black box" theatre (with a flexible stage and seating) should be included to continue the kind of work that was being done in the Bette Oliver theatre. He also supported establishing programs for film and television students.

Don faced a formidable situation. A few months before his arrival, two key members of the Asolo's management (Dick Fallon and Steve Rothman) had resigned, and the managing director, Robert Rosenbaum, had suddenly been fired for allegedly causing the Asolo's projected deficit. Rosenbaum argued that he'd tried "to chart a course and set sail in the middle of all the hurricanes. The best I felt I could do was minimize the damage to the Asolo, get spirits up and make sure the ship didn't sink. Some jumped ship and others were thrown overboard."

There would be a deficit of between $150,000 and $200,000 heading into the 1986–87 season, and the community wondered in which direction the center might go. Creason refused to cast blame for the Asolo's situation. "My job is not to dwell on the problems," he said, "but to get on with solving the problems and getting the job done." His chief concern was to bring stability and order.

Creason's first priority was to increase the number of subscribers and cultivate more corporate support. Fortunately, he had a strong background in marketing. The box office had begun to computerize its operation, and soon they could determine the composition of the Asolo audience. Creason's goal was to cut expenses while preserving the quality of the productions.

John Ulmer approved of the center's new direction. "The board realized the original plan to import famous stars was impractical," he said. "A regional theatre can't exist on the strength of big-name stars brought in from the outside. A theatre has to have its own identity and grow out of what is here." He also looked forward to having a larger mainstage and developing new plays.

A month after Don Creason's appointment there was a "lively" discussion one evening with Gulf Coast Constructors and its consultants. In agreement with Jim Scheurenbrand's observation that they start "from a blank paper as far as the functional design goes," David Staples, the managing director of Theatre Projects, suggested they throw everything out and start over. Apparently, those at the meeting agreed. During the discussion that followed, Staples mentioned the availability of the decorative interior parts of a turn-of-the-century opera house in Dunfermline, Scotland.

"It was really kind of an offhand remark," he said, "but the more we discussed it the better the idea sounded. This community had brought over a European theatre once before, and had a great fondness for it, and why not do it again? The fact that Sarasota was founded by Scots also made it appealing."

The Dunfermline Opera House was designed in the 1890s by theatre manager and architect Ray Johnson; it opened in 1900. At that time, almost

1,000 patrons could be shoehorned into the auditorium. After extensive remodeling in 1921, the seating was reduced to 750.

The opera house closed in 1955 and was used as a furniture store until the late '70s, when developers moved to have it torn down. The Scottish Arts Council instead had the house designated a historical building—but even this couldn't guarantee its preservation. "Before the outer walls were demolished in 1982," reported the *Glasgow Herald*, "all the plasterwork, the ornate cornices, wall panels, friezes, carved box fronts, proscenium, and ceiling arches were carefully cut out and labeled...Even the frontage stone bearing its proud title was rescued and stored, along with some of the plush seating, and packed into a container." (Fortunately, an architect in Edinburgh had made detailed drawings before the opera house was dismantled.) The Dunfermline Opera House had undergone an ordeal similar to that of the little theatre from Asolo, Italy.

Elizabeth Lindsay happened to be vacationing in Edinburgh at this time and took it upon herself to go to Dunfermline and investigate the project's feasibility. She found the parts—which included the front of the balcony, pilasters and capitals—in the trailer of an eighteen-wheeler. After inspecting what was there, she returned home and gave a positive report to the Asolo board. Her efforts and opinion were a major factor in their support of the project.

In Sarasota, Staples's suggestion had growing support from the Asolo board, which felt that importing this Scottish theatre might duplicate something of the charm and tradition of the historic Asolo, "its ambience and intimacy," while at the same time increasing the seating capacity. Robert Wilhelm, now head of the Asolo board's construction committee, said, "At minimal cost, we are getting an exquisite theatre that is going to have a great deal of appeal. If we were to attempt to build from scratch a theatre that had such fine detail and craftsmanship to it, it would be vastly more expensive."

At the September meeting, the Asolo board voted to purchase the opera house's decorative parts for $49,000 plus $18,000 for shipping. The state would pay half the cost; a portion of Burt Reynolds's $1 million pledge would be added to that, and the rest would come from contributions. "People know that this is really going to happen," said Elizabeth Lindsay, who headed the local drive to raise $3.5 million. "We're getting the message across that this is a performing arts center and a major education facility that is going to have an enormous impact on the Sarasota-Manatee community." The theatre parts arrived in November 1986.

Gulf Coast had assembled a world-class construction team. The consultants, Theatre Projects and Stuart Barger, were perfect partners for the venture, and Asolo technical director Victor Meyrich would supervise the theatre's technical requirements during the construction of the center. Some of the decorative parts of the opera house were missing, and it was up to Robert L. Stone, Gulf Coast's project manager, to re-create those elements. He did so by using descriptive reports, drawings of every elevation, photographs and a detailed photometric survey of the interior. "The luxury of this project for us, the architects, is not the budget, or the schedule, or space allowances," said Stuart Barger, "but the wealth of talent that has been brought together."

Vic Meyrich wrote up the architectural plan that described the spaces in the new building, how they would be used and the sort of equipment that might be needed in each space. From this a schematic architectural plan would be created.

In June 1987, Barger was named the sole architect for the ninety-six-thousand-square-foot complex, which, according to the plans, would house the Dunfermline as well as a 150-seat black-box theatre for students and experimental work; classrooms and rehearsal space for the acting conservatory; and a television studio, post-production and editing rooms, a film and tape library, classrooms and other facilities for the new film, TV and recording conservatory program.

Barger had never designed a theatre before and so came in with an open mind. Vic Meyrich and Theatre Projects were able to point him in the right direction, and the theatre, according to those who were engaged in the project, would not have become what it is today without him. He also managed to bring the project in on time and on budget.

After a yearlong search, Lee Warner became Asolo's chief executive officer in the summer of 1987. Warner had been the assistant director of the Florida Division of Historical Resources and had never before run a performing arts organization. Charles Murphy, head of the Asolo search committee, explained, "Our first priority was to find someone with excellent administrative skills. We also wanted someone who had managed a major complex and who would be able to work with the politicians in Tallahassee."

"I was not hired because there was something drastically wrong with the Asolo," said Warner. "That does not suggest that there is not room for improvement." But, he cracked, "Asolo ain't broke, and we ain't gonna fix it." He saw his major challenge as "building a complete program that serves the Sarasota community and a national constituency."

One of the things that had to be done was to build partnerships between corporate interests and theatre. "[Corporate sponsors] may have nothing to do with theatre, but they have a stake in the quality of life in the Tampa Bay area," said Warner. He would make no major changes; the selection of plays, along with other artistic decisions, would be left to artistic director John Ulmer. "I was a bureaucrat for a long time," Warner admitted, "and the single most important thing I learned was bureaucrats don't know everything."

Soon afterward, the state Board of Regents approved a program allowing FSU to grant a master's degree in film, with some involvement from the University of South Florida. (They also approved planning for a bachelor's degree in film to be granted by the University of Central Florida in Orlando, where MCA and Disney were building studios.)

Warner promised not to rush the move into the new complex, insisting the company wait until every aspect—dressing rooms, technical equipment, etc.—had been completed. But he did say that he expected to light a Christmas tree in the building by December 1988.

But first there would have to be a farewell season in the historic Asolo, and then plans for an appropriate inaugural season in the new complex. Warner hoped the national theatre industry would pay attention to the transition. His primary goal had a familiar ring to it: "To take the Asolo from regional to national recognition."

On the evening of January 6, 1988, a group of about sixty people—actors, stage managers, costumers, technicians, secretaries and management—gathered at nearby New College to celebrate the beginning of the Asolo Center's construction. Painted shovels were passed out to signify how long each person had been with the theatre, with gold presented to the three Asolo employees with the longest tenures: Bob Naismith, Marian and me. The next morning that same group, joined by dignitaries like state senator Robert Johnson (who had helped secure a $5.5 million appropriation form the state legislature), reassembled to use those shovels to break ground on a plot of land between the Ringling Museum and U.S. 41.

The struggle to raise money for the new facility eased toward the end of the year, when the Kresge Foundation of Michigan approved a $250,000 challenge grant for the $10 million project (of which the Asolo would be required to raise $796,148). Elizabeth Lindsay, now chairman of the fundraising committee, touted it as "the largest foundation grant we've received, and it's from a prestigious foundation that is known for studying its

ASOLO

ASOLO PERFORMING ARTS CENTER, INC.

Spring 1988

There are no bad seats in this house!

In a little over a year, the new Asolo Performing Arts Center will be a reality in Sarasota and, if you're like me, you can't wait for the opening!

The Center campaign for private support is well underway and construction has begun, but our work is not completed. We still need the support of many patrons and friends if we are to reach our goal.

The "Buy-A-Seat" campaign is an excellent opportunity to invest in the cultural life of this community, support the Asolo Performing Arts Center and receive lasting recognition for your gift. As the enclosed brochure details, your gift not only supports the Asolo and provides you with permanent recognition of your generosity but also enters your name for a fabulous list of prizes!

The new Asolo will be magnificent. Please join us by considering your gift of $1000, $500 or $250 today.

See you at the Asolo!

Burt Reynolds

Burt Reynolds

Postal Drawer E • Sarasota, Florida 34230 • 813 952-0688

grant applications extremely carefully. A grant from them can only enhance the project's credibility."

But the money problems would not go away. After the merger with The Theatre Inc. created the Performing Arts Center, dealing with the various boards and trying to make the new organization work had produced a situation that was somewhat "complicated," as Linda DiGabriele, then the Asolo's managing director, described it. There was a need now to streamline the theatre's

Eric Tarvares, Mary Proctor and Robert Patteri in Rostand's *Cyrano de Bergerac*, the final production in the historic Asolo. *Photo by Gary W. Sweetman.*

fundraising efforts, and so it was proposed that the boards of directors of the Festival Association and the Asolo Performing Arts Center agree to merge. This would simplify things for prospective donors, some of whom were confused when requests for contributions were made by two separate organizations. The merger was made in April 1989, and the move for efficiency would in time pay off. Lee Warner was given credit for calming the waters and successfully bringing the two boards together. "Now we are going to be one family working together," he said. Some cite this as his greatest achievement during his time at the Asolo.

The headline read, "Curtain falls, so do tears at Asolo finale." *Cyrano de Bergerac* had been chosen specifically to end the historic Asolo's final season. And it was true that after the final curtain call for *Cyrano de Bergerac*, audience members and some performers couldn't hold back the tears. "I started crying this afternoon," Tracy Newsome told me. Tracy had been the Asolo's house manager and "bell ringer" for eighteen years. "There are so many memories wrapped up in this place." Indeed, in that space, hundreds of actors had performed in more than three hundred plays over a span of almost thirty years.

The parting was almost ritualistic: that final audience, together with Asolo actors, technicians and staff, formed a torchlight procession that made its way to the new theatre. The crowd buzzed with excitement. Those present

Marian and Brad Wallace on the historic Asolo stage after the final curtain call, July 30, 1989.

included Charles Reed, chancellor of the university system of Florida; Bernard F. Sliger, president of the Florida State University; Gil Lazier, dean of the FSU School of Theatre; and other state and local dignitaries.

There on the new stage, John Ulmer raised a toast to the Asolo's future: "You are this theatre's first audience. The first of thousands of people who will come here…We have a mandate to produce in this building art and beauty, education and enlightenment and joy. Come back again. You haven't heard anything yet." Chick Austin might have raised the same toast.

Eb Thomas felt that the celebration should have been more balanced, that more focus should have been given to the historic Asolo:

> *This was, I think, the most significant development in the entire 200-plus years of the Asolo Theatre's existence. What had been a quaint attraction located inside a castle in a relatively small hill town about 50 miles northwest of Venice was revived in the mid 1950s like the Phoenix springing forth from its own ashes. And in its new incarnation it was not only admired as a treasure in itself but became the site of a thriving theatrical enterprise. We sometimes forget that the little jewel box, for all its splendid history, first truly came to life inside a rather unimpressive building just west of the Ringling Museum in Sarasota, Florida. Consider the fact that the Asolo Theatre Company, from 1960–1989, probably presented at least 500 times more performances than had been given in the theatre during the entire first 160 years of its life.*

The Asolo Theatre Festival's first installment: July 12, 1960–July 29, 1989.

Chapter 11

Brand-New Directions

It's important for the audience to know that there is a home plate.
—*Margaret Booker*

In May, the Asolo Performing Arts Center Inc. was renamed the Asolo Center for the Performing Arts Inc., with the idea that the new name better described the institution as a whole and would help distinguish it from venues that only booked touring shows.

During the fall, Lee Blessing's *A Walk in the Woods* served as a "warm-up" for the mainstage. The set had been left on stage for the center's impressive grand opening on January 20, 1990.

The dedication ceremony began at 2:30 p.m., when Asolo board president William Strode welcomed the almost one thousand patrons outside the building's main entrance. After State Senator Robert Johnson (a member of the national council for the arts) spoke, Strode and Secretary of State Jim Smith cut the ribbon. The Asolo Center for the Performing Arts was officially open.

John Ulmer led the dedication of the Asolo mainstage, which was to be known as the Harold E. and Esther M. Mertz Theatre. (Esther Mertz had made a major contribution to the building fund in memory of her late husband.) After remarks by Timothy Mason, director of the Scottish Arts Council, the ribbon to the mainstage was cut by Mertz and James C. Cameron, provost of Dunfermline, Scotland. "This is rather a sad occasion for Scotland, which has lost the opera house forever," Mason later admitted. "But as in the fairy tale, at least now the sleeping beauty can go to the ball." The afternoon's ceremony concluded with a performance by the Kiltie Pipers and Highland Dancers from Sarasota's Riverview High School.

The Harold E. and Esther M. Mertz Theater at the FSU Center for the Performing Arts. *Photo by Wayne Eastep.*

A black-tie audience returned that evening for a 7:30 opening performance of G.B. Shaw's *Man and Superman*. Afterward, Burt Reynolds and his wife, Lonnie Anderson, cut the ribbon for the center's film and television wing, which was named in his honor. "This is a majestic, beautiful theatre, and I'm absolutely thrilled to be a part of it," he said. "I had a feeling of déjà vu walking onto this [sound]stage. It reminds me of rehearsals for *Playhouse 90* in the old days of live television." Reynolds also expressed a desire to teach there, saying, "It's one of the things I think I do well."

Some aspects of the night, however, were at odds with the festivities. John Ulmer had referred to the completion of the center as "a miracle" and went on to say, "We're going to need another miracle; a miracle so that a producing organization can be built to fill this great building with great theatre." Dick Fallon was not invited to take part in the program. But he was in the audience and later called it "a dream come true." He received a standing ovation at the opening night's performance.

In an editorial, the *Sarasota Herald-Tribune* praised "such enthusiasts as indefatigable fund-raiser Elizabeth Lindsay, legislator/arts patron Robert Johnson, Arvida president Bob Wilhelm, who oversaw construction; Asolo board of directors president Bill Strode, executive director Lee Warner, and artistic director John Ulmer. All deserve stage front recognition for their faith, vision and downright hard work."

A nationally touring Asolo production had been an annual occurrence—and a profitable one—throughout the '80s. *Blithe Spirit* opened the Asolo's "great winter tour," as we jokingly referred to it, on December 28, 1989. We played in New England, upstate New York, Michigan and Iowa in January and February.

During the summer of 1990, the board announced that the Asolo would buy out the final two years of John Ulmer's contract. There were various reasons for his dismissal. A new musical based on Carlo Goldoni's *A Servant of Two Masters* was being written by John Ulmer and composer David Bernetti and was to close the 1990–91 season. But the production was cancelled because it would be too expensive. Frustrated, John argued that without the musical, there would be no new works in the season, and this, he said, "holds no interest for me." There were also reports of a "long, bitter clash" with Lee Warner. Warner, however, insisted that John's leaving was not due to any personal conflict between the two. The Asolo board supported Warner's position.

Shortly before the announcement was made, John Ulmer invited me over one evening to voice his frustrations with the situation over chocolate pie. The acrimony surprised me. Up to that point, the conflicts had remained behind closed doors.

There were strong feelings—both pro and con—among the staff and in the community regarding John Ulmer's departure. "I'm very saddened by John's leaving," said Paula Twitchell, a former head of the Asolo Guild. "I am concerned that there are persons in authority who are not theater people and who do not hold excellent theater as the foremost object." Lola Hanna, a longtime and generous Asolo supporter, resigned from the Asolo Board, saying she thought John Ulmer had been treated badly, "and I just don't like the direction things are going."

An employee who had been privy to the decision-making process anonymously summed up the other side's view: John Ulmer "wasn't the strong leader that the artistic side needed," he said. "He couldn't articulate a clear artistic vision. He was indecisive and he had no head for budgets. I know that, as artistic director, that didn't have to be his main concern, but he needed to have a better grasp of the financial end of things. I don't think Warner was out to get him. John was his own worst enemy."

My wife, Marian, by then a seasoned veteran as production stage manager, took a more balanced position. "People are demoralized," she said at the time. "The struggle between the artistic staff and the administration has been hard. There are no villains here, in my mind. It's just an unfortunate situation. We need a cheerleader."

But even in a town made famous by the circus, none was to be found.

The new artistic director was expected to be chosen by January 1991. Lee Warner brought in George Kandel, a partner in Management Consultants for the Arts, to help pare down the long list of candidates. Finally, in late July, three finalists made the cut. There were two men and one woman, but their names were not released. Lee Warner assured supporters that A) none of the three candidates wanted to "radically change the Asolo's direction or the kind of plays it produces"; B) each wanted to produce a broad spectrum of plays including the classics and new material; and C) each pledged to utilize the acting conservatory. The search committee, according to Kandel, insisted "the candidate had to be committed to at least a few months of rotating repertory [per season],…sees theater's place in the community, [and] is capable of creating a body of work that says something to a community."

The announcement occurred on October 19: the Asolo's new artistic director would be Margaret Booker. At forty-eight, Megs Booker had an impressive résumé. While still a young woman, she'd received a Fulbright fellowship to study in Sweden under Ingmar Bergman, who, in addition to his film accomplishments, was also a passionate and accomplished stage director. A graduate of Stanford University, she had been artistic director at Seattle's Intiman Theatre (which she founded) and the Hartman Theatre Company in Stamford, Connecticut (which closed during her tenure). As a freelance director, she had worked at the Cleveland Playhouse, the Williamstown Theatre Festival in Massachusetts, the Eugene O'Neill National Playwright's Conference in Connecticut, the Yale Repertory, the McCarter Theater, the Oregon Shakespeare Festival and several European theatres. She also had been named a *TIME* magazine "Newsmaker of Tomorrow."

Lee Warner praised Booker's "energy, intelligence, promise and dynamism" and ranked the decision as one of the most significant steps in the Asolo's history. "In Margaret Booker," said Elizabeth Lindsay, "we found interests and philosophy consistent with the committee's direction." State Senator Robert Johnson said Booker was the "critical building block to complete the Asolo project that began several years ago."

For her part, Booker felt that over the years the Asolo may have restricted its play selection in an effort to please an older audience. But, she said, advanced age "doesn't mean that the audience isn't sharp. The idea that life is over or that you have to cater to the most conservative interests just isn't true." She said that she had been "weaned" on the classics, and these proven works would be used to create a sense of stability. "It's important for the audience to know that there is a home plate, a first base and so on," she explained. "If they know they've got some secure places, then they'll go to the wild outfield with you. They'll play ball." She outlined a balance between the classics (Shakespeare, Shaw, etc.) and modern plays (recent New York productions and premieres of new plays), the latter to constitute about 40 percent of each season.

"Executive director Lee Warner, whose stated goal is to put Asolo on the national map, has said that a special fundraising campaign is being mounted to raise money for heightened artistic costs," wrote Porter Anderson in the *Tampa Tribune*.

"It may take five years for Asolo to attract national attention for consistently strong work," Booker estimated, but its mission, "in blunt terms, is to create the most exciting work on stage that you can."

Her tenure with the Asolo began in the fall of 1990. Marian adapted well to the new regime; I wouldn't work at the Asolo again for the next three years.

In November, members of the first Asolo film conservatory class took three top prizes in the Alamo Student Film Competition at the Fort Lauderdale Film Festival.[2] Stuart Kaminsky pointed out that these entries were only class projects; even better results could be expected when the thesis projects were submitted the next year.

Less than a month into the job, Booker's leadership style was evident. "Booker is coming across in the Asolo corridors as an energetic and straightforward woman who pulls no punches and who expects others to share her enthusiasm and her high standards," as Charlie Huisking described her.

The dynamic Booker had already captivated Sarasota with her whirlwind activity—auditioning actors both locally and in other parts of the state, sitting in on rehearsals for Asolo mainstage productions and reading countless new plays. Even her wardrobe was fodder for local wags. "Suits and dresses?"

2. *and the home of the brave*, directed by Matt Stevens, took first place in the narrative category; Curtis Petree's *Josiah's Secret* took first place in the feature-length screenplay category; and *Inside the Mind's Eye*, directed by Donna Wheeler, took first place in the documentary category.

wrote Louise Bruderle for *West Coast Woman.* "Nope, she'd rather have on jeans and sweats, her wavy brown hair spilling over her shoulders as she gestures."

Under Booker, the Asolo was immediately taking a new direction, and there would be no apologies. "Those who are not able to adapt mentally," she said, "and do what we really have to—which is to create an incredibly positive-oriented collaborative place—may not make it through the transition."

Booker believed the role of regional theatre was to "give voice to an area and to our country." Regional theatre also allowed a producer to plan long-range for a new work and find the right director, actors and technicians. "There's basically nothing getting developed on Broadway," she once said in an interview. "In the last ten years, all the Pulitzer Prize plays were developed in a regional theater."

The 1991–92 season would include more adventurous works, plays largely unfamiliar to the Asolo audience. The opener was a relatively small new musical, *Svengali* ("big" musicals, Booker had said, would always be beyond the Asolo's resources). *Lost Electra*, a new play by Asolo literary manager Bruce Rodgers, would follow. In the future, Booker wanted to do some very controversial plays and hoped eventually to have a second stage for workshopping. (The new building contained space for a second stage—though its completion had been delayed—but this was to be dedicated to the conservatory.)

In selecting plays for a season, Booker said, she first looked for "the quality of writing" and "a unique voice. The kind of writing that has something to say about the concerns of our times and what it means to us now." She promised to choose plays that would require the best talent available. "I hope to draw people of stature to the Asolo."

"Guest directors," she declared, "must be at least as good as I am." She was particularly excited that London's Anthony Cornish had been contracted for an upcoming season to direct *The Man of Mode*, a revival of an English Restoration play by Sir George Etherege. She was also "thrilled" that New York City's Oz Scott would be directing *Fences*, a Pulitzer Prize– and Tony Award–winning play.

It was estimated that $200,000 needed to be added to the artistic budget for the coming year.

Stemming from her national ambitions, Booker had developed reservations regarding the Asolo rotating repertory system. "I'm not sure a resident talent pool is able to do it [produce a high-quality theatre season]. The difficulty is in attracting those people to stay here that length of time, because they're also working in television and movies." Of 250 Florida actors who auditioned for her, Booker felt only 4 or 5 were suitable. (John Ulmer quipped privately, "Even if it's true, you don't say it.")

"I like repertory," Booker said, "but I have to have a high level of talent, and if that means they eliminate each other, a decision has to be made." On this matter, she showed shades of John Ulmer. She had no reservations about her mission. "I was hired to give this theater a national profile," she said. "I was hired to raise the level of work here." The board was delighted; Booker felt she was earning trust and support.

"The Asolo is in a period of transition," Lee Warner had said upon Megs Booker's hiring, "changing from a small theater of limited scope to one with an expanded program and national ambition." And as with many transitions, there was always the possibility of political and monetary pitfalls.

Warner was concerned about the 1991 recession and frustrated because he couldn't predict what its effect would be on the Asolo, or when the economy might rebound. The Asolo planned to cut its budget by $200,000, but the "artistic product"—including the $200,000 Booker had added to the budget for the hiring of actors, directors and designers—would not be affected. The first three shows of the 1990–91 season, all selected by John Ulmer before he was removed, had been playing to only 55 percent of capacity. His new musical, *The Servant of Two Masters*, had already been cut from the season. In an attempt to stimulate public interest, his penultimate choice, *Dracula*, was also nixed.

In January, the deficit for 1990–91 was projected between $100,000 and $300,000, dependent on what steps were taken to control it. In August, it was announced that the deficit had reached $369,000 and that the Asolo owed more than $4 million. Most of the debt lay in the $3.3 million still owed for the new building's construction loans. (There were also other bank loans and a $500,000 line of credit from the FSU Foundation.)

Paid attendance had dropped from 86,230 in the 1989–90 season to 68,763 in 1990–91, and box office revenues were down to $1.2 million from $1.5 million. Still, Warner felt that sufficient increases in donations and box office revenue could be achieved to make the Asolo debt-free in three years.

For various reasons, and despite the recession Warner feared, other performing arts companies in Sarasota fared much better. According to financial reports, the Sarasota Ballet of Florida had collected $100,000 more in ticket revenue than anticipated, and the Van Wezel Performing Arts Hall recorded a string of sold-out performances. A production of *Evita* by the Players of Sarasota was, at the time, the largest-grossing show in that theatre's history. After a slow period earlier that winter. Elizabeth Kareg, chief executive of the Players, explained, "If you have a good show, people will come out even in bad times."

Lee Warner remained steadfast that the Asolo was the only arts institution in Sarasota that "through its own efforts has undertaken to become nationally significant."

But members of the arts community in Sarasota began to express concerns about what they felt were inflated ambitions regarding national recognition. There were also questions about Booker's attitude, in addition to her aims.

In a letter to the editor, K.T. Curran, a local actress, wrote:

> *If Ms. Booker did, in fact, truly wish to raise the artistic quality in Florida…she would make an effort to really get to know local theatre people. She would visit area theatres and exchange and share ideas in interviews that last longer than five minutes. She would recognize that the attitude which places New York actors on a pedestal will never build ensemble work—work that grows out of the souls of the actors committed to a community and appreciated by that community.*

Chapter 12

Feast and Famine

I'm not the only one to get the impression that we are to believe that the Asolo began with its new building. Indeed, it has seemed most of this year that the Asolo might end *with its new building.*
—Eric Tavares

There were two significant additions to the Asolo Conservatory in the fall of 1991. First, the two-year program was expanded to three years (the 1991 first-year students would be the first to have a third year). However, those in authority still weren't quite sure what would be taught—and how—in that third year.

The second addition, an early '80s conservatory graduate named Brant Pope, was hired by Gil Lazier as the director of the Asolo's professional actor training program. After studying in Sarasota, Brant had served as artistic director of Michigan's Festival Playhouse and had substantial credits as a director and teacher. "No MFA program in the country can touch us," he said. "We have a tremendous conservatory. We have a direct relationship with a [regional] theatre and we have a film conservatory that trains our students for acting in television and film."

Brant had already been working with Stuart Kaminsky on joint projects for the theatre and film conservatories. "Frankly, it's distressing that the Asolo has not developed the national reputation it ought to have," said Brant. "Where I want to change our identity is as a producing organization." What he envisioned were student productions of classic plays and new works—training that would take them beyond the classroom to work before an audience.

Booker's plan, he soon discovered, was slightly different. "My commitment," she said, "is that the second-year students understudy, and in the third year every student goes on stage at least once [either in a speaking role or as an extra]." Brant wanted the third-year students to become associate members of the professional company.

The two also differed in their attitudes toward tradition. Booker envisioned a brave new world—a complete break from the past—whereas Brant had a high regard for the people he'd known as a student. He planned to bring back "familiar faces" from past seasons, company members such as Isa Thomas, Bob Strane and Eb Thomas. Brant said, "I want to provide something of the old theatre for the people who feel alienated by the changes that happened to the Asolo. And it would be great for the students to work with these talented people."

Dean Gil Lazier announced that an additional 161-seat proscenium theatre, also located in the Asolo Center, was set to open in 1994. (The original idea for a black-box theatre had been scrapped.) Architect Stuart Barger described the theatre as a "flexible, intimate place, with excellent sightlines and acoustics, that features the actor." The new theatre, named for Jane B. Cook, would be used primarily by the FSU/Asolo Conservatory.

In early December, Bob Strane returned to the Asolo to direct a student production of Shakespeare's *Twelfth Night*. Appropriately, it was performed in the theatre named for one of the Asolo's greatest talents, Bette Oliver. In a grand reunion with Bob, I played Sir Toby Belch, and my youngest daughter also appeared as a servant in the production. It brought back memories of very successful years.

I should reiterate the previously cited thoughts of two writers regarding the Educational Enrichment Tour (which had faded away in the '70s). Henry Hewes, writing in the *Saturday Review* in 1967, felt it was "in the national interest" to investigate how such tours could increase future audiences and better arts education. In 1966, Warren Cato, director of the Theatre Guild, called the tour "the most exciting program in theatre for secondary school children in the country."

The Asolo, as was said before, received a grant from the federal government that enabled the company to make a huge leap forward in 1966. As Dick Fallon said to me, "That grant and the touring program made it possible to operate the Asolo year-round and become in that year [1966] a fully professional Equity company. We began receiving from the state primarily

From left: Playwright Susan Zeder, Barbara Bush and Linda DiGabriele at the Kennedy Center.

because of the school touring program. For many, many years my argument to continue and increase state support was the success of the school tour."

(The national tour had been launched in 1982. Over the next several years, it produced a profit for the Asolo.)

And then there was an elementary school project called the Tours for Young Audiences.

Linda DiGabriele, since coming to the Asolo in 1973, had served at times as the company's administrative director, director of touring programs and stage manager and had orchestrated twenty-six regional and national tours for the Asolo mainstage and educational companies. (Linda had also served on a number of national panels and advisory boards, including the executive committee for the League of Resident Theatres (LORT), an advisory panel for the National Endowment for the Arts and the John F. Kennedy Theatre for Young Audiences.) During her time as director of the Asolo Tours for Young Audiences, two of that program's shows played at the Kennedy Center in Washington, D.C., and at the Brooklyn Academy of Music.

The Asolo was responsible for the oldest continuously operating school touring programs in the country playing before more than two million people in twenty-six years. In 1975, both the Educational Enrichment tour and the Actors-in-the-Schools tour were discontinued. In 1990, the national tour was discontinued. And in 1992, the Tours for Young Audiences were discontinued. Budgetary problems were cited as justification.

All three finalists for the artistic director position had pledged no radical changes. Only after taking the job did Booker reveal that repertory and a resident company did not fit into her plans. Now, in 1992, she told the board that she'd heard of the Asolo touring companies before she had heard of the performing arts center, and this, she felt, was a case of the cart coming before the horse. She was getting rid of the national tours, she explained, because she felt the productions were of poor quality. But until then, the Asolo had always been a national leader in the production of these programs.

Local media praised Booker's first season.

The *Pelican*:

> *Asolo has a lovely problem. They've got a hit on their hands with the musical* Svengali *which has box-office lines jammed.*

Bradenton Herald:

> *Asolo's* Svengali *production headed for Broadway. Gross receipts for single ticket sales* [during a recent week] *have been the equivalent of a full house every day.*

Tampa Times:

> Svengali*'s spell is indeed strong.*

Tampa Times:

> Remembrance *never lets its viewers forget that love sometimes can conquer all. This brilliant production captures honestly the heartache and hatred that must be overcome along the way.*

Sarasota Herald-Tribune:

> Sweet and Hot *is a swingin' celebration.*

Bradenton Herald:

> *Harold Arlen's* Sweet and Hot *is an Asolo gem. Boyd* [the director] *kept things moving along at such a brisk pace that the show just flew by and ended sooner than I would have liked.*

No doubt, Booker was changing the Asolo's image. In addition to Anthony Cornish, she had contracted Hal Prince, a major Broadway director, to direct a premiere of *The Petrified Prince*. Prince had won nineteen Tony Awards; his credits included *Cabaret*, *Fiddler on the Roof*, *Sweeney Todd* and *Phantom of the Opera*. "Prince approached us because he'd heard about the level of the work being done here," said Lee Warner. "It would be a big step forward in achieving national recognition."

Booker was staging multigenerational work and trying to showcase African American and Hispanic playwrights—an effort to generate an audience base from demographics that had not been tapped in Sarasota. The view was that theatre had always been oriented toward the snowbird population and "had not done enough for the local community." And now, to be fair, the local community *was* excited.

It seemed, however, that problems were developing. By 1993, the conflicts between Booker's agenda and that of FSU were becoming more pronounced; Booker was perceived as uninterested in the conservatory students. "As partners, both FSU and the Asolo contribute to the artistic vision that defines the Asolo," said Brant Pope. "Both sides passionately care about the Asolo, but there's a philosophical difference about what will help the theatre and the conservatory prosper. From our perspective, the fact that not one student has played a major role in a mainstage show in the last three years is evidence of that philosophical difference." Booker pointed out that she had used students in *King Lear* and planned to cast them in the Hal Prince production. "I'm talking about the quality of roles, not the quantity," countered Pope. "It's not enough to be cast as townspeople or spear carriers."

Also by 1993, budget concerns at the Asolo had degenerated into a fog of contradictions:

- In 1992, FSU had become owner of the Asolo Center, which, in exchange, allowed the university to retire Asolo's debt to them of $3.4 million.

But the Asolo was still in debt to vendors and others and more deeply in debt than most regional theatres.

- Paid attendance increased from 57 percent in 1991–92 to 70 percent of capacity in 1992–93.

Meanwhile, money donated to the theatre the previous season had fallen $600,000 short of the Asolo's goal.

- Lee Warner insisted, "We're not an institution that is sinking; we're an institution that is rising. We have turned a financial corner… We're reducing our long-term debt."

But the Asolo was spending $300,000 more per season on productions than during the Ulmer years. (Murmurs suggested that Megs Booker, like John Ulmer, had no patience with preparing a budget.) The theatre was forced to deal on a cash-only basis with some suppliers who would no longer grant the Asolo credit.

- The Asolo had lost 600 Angels in the last two years but gained 1,800 new ones during the same period.

The public's relationship with the Asolo was also having its ups and downs.

Warner voiced the philosophy, "Doing significant work in a national context has one precondition—you have to satisfy your local audience." But there was a recurring complaint that production values outshone the acting and the quality of the scripts.

"Booker isn't trying to meet the needs of this audience," one detractor said privately. "She's only interested in doing multicultural and highly conceptual productions that will get her on the cover of national theatre magazines." But another patron, Lenora Just, said of Booker, "I really think she's on the cutting edge. I'm glad we became subscribers."

John Ulmer admitted, "Megs has done what I should have done. She says, 'This is what it will cost, so go find the money.'"

Eric Tavares had been a leading actor with the Asolo company from 1983 to 1990, including the title role in *Cyrano de Bergerac*, the final Asolo production in the old theatre. In a letter to the editor during Booker's reign, Eric wrote:

> *I resent, and I think I am speaking for many others, the implication that the Asolo was a sleepy little semi-professional theatre where happy plays for one's maiden aunt was the rule…Growth is, of course, necessary and must be nourished by the community. But I'm not the only one to get the impression that we are to believe that the Asolo began with its new building. Indeed, it has seemed most of this year that the Asolo might* end *with its new building.*

Local reviewers joined the growing criticism. Booker had eagerly welcomed London's Anthony Cornish to the Asolo to direct *Man of Mode*. But the reviews were far from glowing: "Beautifully presented and splendidly performed by a large cast," wrote the *Lakeland Ledger*, "*Man of Mode* purports to heap ridicule upon the attitudes and behavior of the rich. This objective, however worthy it may seem to some, cannot save this handsome production from being a crushing bore. Ample evidence of this came when about half the substantial audience on the Saturday night I saw the show did not return after intermission." The run crew made a game of standing in the lobby at intermission to count the departing audience members.

For the Christmas holiday production of 1993, Booker commissioned playwright Phil Bosakowski to create a circus-themed play "for all ages"; Booker would direct the premiere of the show, entitled *Big Top!*. "See the Fabulous Flying Farinas and their human cannonball act!" the flyer shouted. "Thrill to clowns, animal trainers, web girls and gorillas! Live the wild, wacky world of Sarasota's circus heritage!"

The first preview before the *Big Top!* opening had been sold to the *Sarasota Herald-Tribune*, which was using the occasion for a special company celebration. Before the performance began, an Asolo employee came out on state to explain that the script was unfinished; the audience would see the first act only. (Among Asolo insiders, rumors circulated that the playwright was not particularly fond of the circus to begin with, leaving the impression that he was dragging his feet on the project.)

By opening night, both acts were finished (more or less). But after the opening, reviewers pulled no punches.

Tampa Tribune:

> Big Top! *Turns out to be a Big Flop…*[The show] *cost about $180,000 to stage. What's the problem here? The true responsibility lies with the Asolo's artistic director and the play's director, Margaret Booker.*

Sarasota Herald-Tribune:

> *Colorful* Big Top! *collapses from the ground up. The cast lacks the personality one associates with the circus. As directed by Margaret Booker, they're cardboard characters who don't make us believe that they actually have anything to do with the circus…But once again at the Asolo, the production values come off better than the play, although this time, there's not much of a play to compete.*

St. Petersburg Times:

> Big Top!*: It's a circus. This contrived and bizarre play at the Asolo spins out of control.* Big Top! *is a complete fiasco from its wrongheaded conception to the forced bravado of the exclamation point in its title. Commissioned by the Asolo Theatre to write a play about the circus, Phil Bosakowski came up with an inept mutation of Arthur Miller and* Animal Kingdom. *Though audiences are shunning* Big Top! *like the plague, connoisseurs of disaster will want to check it out…Now the theater is stuck with a bomb for the holidays, following a lackluster* King Lear, *also directed by Booker.*

The season might still have been saved: Hal Prince had been booked to direct a premiere at the Asolo. Having someone of his stature would have been a coup for Booker—to show the critics that the theatre could extend beyond regional constraints—and a balm for previous missteps.

But in mid-November, the show was cancelled. The producer explained that the second act wouldn't be ready in time.

Charlie Husking summed up the Asolo's dilemma: "Is a cutting-edge theater with national ambitions realistic in a retirement and resort community like Sarasota, where corporations and wealthy arts patrons are bombarded with requests from competing organizations?" The answer at this time was more and more a resounding "no."

According to one Asolo staff member, "[Booker] did not embrace the acting company, the staff or the community. Had she had a relationship with the community, she might have been able to sell her agenda." Indeed, I had next to no firsthand experience with Megs Booker; most of the Asolo's resident actors had been forced to find work elsewhere during her tenure.

In December 1993, the Asolo Theatre board elected not to renew Margaret Booker's contract.

Chapter 13

New York Critics Don't Fund Regional Theatres

The leaders now had a new though perhaps subliminal goal; to achieve for their theatres a central place and so to influence the future rather than simply preserving the past
—Joseph Zeigler, Regional Theatre: the Revolutionary Stage

"National recognition" is a watchword throughout the Asolo's history. Early on, praise spread nationwide for the manner in which the theatre served its region. In the '60s and '70s, the Asolo received glowing reviews from newspapers and magazines from Boston to Miami. But those yearning for national recognition had overlooked the nature of this praise and turned instead to almost any means to gain attention.

Indeed, later attempts to gain national attention by breaking new theatrical ground resulted in, at best, national criticism and, at worst, borderline bankruptcy. The Asolo of the '80s, especially, had clearly marked the pitfalls that regional theatre faces in any place and time.

In 1980, the Asolo had produced a new play entitled *Transcendental Love* by Daryl Boylan. The play dealt with the life of Ralph Waldo Emerson and his relationship with Margaret Fuller. After a run in Sarasota, a New York producer (Frank Gero, father-in-law to Liza Minnelli) managed to take the show to the city for the Asolo's first premiere performance there. The critics were neither amused nor impressed, and their disgust was too easily linked to the Asolo.

Kevin Kelly of the *Boston Globe*:

> *It's an insult to Emerson and everyone else...If Boylan's play represents Asolo, then regional theater is in far worse trouble than I had thought.*

Frank Rich of the *New York Times*:

> *A series of romantic and comic interludes that stretch inanity to the point of absurdity…The show has been imported from Florida and is billed as the first New York production of the Asolo State Theatre in the theater's 20-year history. I look forward to seeing another sample of this playhouse's work in the year 2000.*

Marylyn Stasio of the *New York Post*:

> *An import from Sarasota, Fla., the Asolo State Theatre production manages to make a TV sitcom out of the domestic and literary affairs of Ralph Waldo Emerson.*

John Simon of *New York Magazine* called it a "horror" deserving an "ultimate booby prize." It belonged, he wrote, "in one of New York's theaters as alligators in the city's sewers."

In April 1986, the premiere of *Forgive Me, Evelyn Buns* opened at the Asolo. The play was directed by Alan Arkin and included his wife, Barbara Dana, and sons Adam and Anthony Arkin in the cast. Porter Anderson, a graduate of the Asolo Conservatory who would later become the critic for Manhattan's *Village Voice*, wrote a *Tampa Tribune* review representative of widespread reaction: "This is not the state theater that our area has nurtured for a generation, nor is it responsible new-play development. If *Buns*—with its incense-sickly story of an obsessed woman who wants good karma—is the prototype the Theatre Inc. claim it is, then they're pointing Asolo in the direction of tawdry, light-as curry-powder sitcoms." That, unfortunately, was national recognition.

"The development of the regional theatre can be viewed as a series of three spiraling thrusts," wrote Joseph Zeigler in his book, *Regional Theatre: The Revolutionary Stage*, and the three, he said, were overlapping. The first of these was *stability*. "The stability thrust was characterized by the overriding concern of each theatre for its own survival and security." The Asolo had certainly experienced this in the financial crises of the '60s and early '70s, and from this there had emerged full houses and the pressing need for a larger performance space. The next thrust was *quality*. Now that the theatre did not have to worry as much about survival, more attention could be paid to the merits of the plays produced. And finally there was *centrality*: what did the rest of the world think about the Asolo? "The leaders now had a new though perhaps subliminal goal: to achieve for their theatres a central place and so to influence the future rather than simply preserving the past."

Stability grew into quality, which was recognized when the Asolo was chosen for the nationally televised production of *The Patriots* and the filming of a play featuring Helen Hayes. But something began to happen in the '80s, and the Asolo became more and more entangled in an effort to rush the thrust of centrality. Judgment became clouded, and a smooth transition from quality to centrality was never allowed to happen. The theatre was forced to go to the back of the line to try and reestablish its stability.

Keep in mind the critique written by William Glover of the Associated Press in 1972: "As everyone from the Keys to Pensacola knows, Asolo…is Florida's official state theatre, and *an exceptional example of regional dramatic enterprise.* [my emphasis]" Other national publications, as noted before, attested during those early years that the Asolo was succeeding in meeting the needs of the people of its region. But those accomplishments were overlooked or ignored, bringing the theatre to the brink of closing. After some maturing, impressing the New York critics can be a legitimate goal. However, New York critics don't fund regional theatres, and if regional supporters get the impression that they are second-class citizens, they will reduce or eliminate their support. Without understanding the implications of "national recognition" for a regional theatre, it can be like fissionable material: it can do great good or great harm.

There is nothing to be gained by laying blame on any individual or group. Every move made during the '80s and '90s was made in a sincere effort to benefit the Asolo and the state of Florida. Still, the blame game would be played en masse.

The Asolo's staff felt, and they were not alone, that Lee Warner's micromanagement had produced unnecessary conflict and that the center was not well administered. Late in March 1994, Warner met with the Asolo board to announce he would resign his position as executive director by July 1.

Warner's resignation fueled the debate as to who bore the responsibility for the Asolo's dilemma. Some continued to blame Megs Booker because her choice of plays, directors and actors undermined the public's confidence. Furthermore, the visual aspects of the productions, while usually spectacular, were financially unjustified when the quality of plays and the acting were subpar. Others pointed to Warner himself because he attempted to hide the reality of the Asolo's situation. Brant Pope charged Warner with a "pattern of deception meant to mask the real nature of the Asolo's problems." Board member Ron Greenbaum said, "Lee led us down the primrose path, and many of us were pretty angry about it. It was like peeling layers of an onion to get the real story. The income projections he gave us weren't based on reality." Warner contended he had always been forthcoming with the board, and Elizabeth Lindsay, among others, backed him up.

Other fingers pointed at the board itself and the push for national recognition. The *Herald-Tribune* felt that the problem lay with board members "who didn't exercise proper oversight and who were caught up in a dream of achieving national and international prominence for what had been a small, beloved institution." One member of Asolo management said, "The board seemed to believe that if the Asolo got famous enough, Brink's trucks from the National Endowment for the Arts would start showing up."

Charlie Husking summoned a Shakespearean level of drama to characterize the recent progression of mistakes. "It's a compelling tale involving bold ventures, towering ambitions and shattered dreams. The principal players are passionate, dedicated well-intentioned people. But some of them have been described as arrogant, out-of-touch and irresponsible. Now they are all hoping this story won't have a tragic ending."

The Asolo was facing a crisis unlike any it had dealt with in the past. In 1968 and 1971, there were questions as to whether the Asolo could survive its financial woes. In those times, the supporters were confident that the theatre management was not to blame and were willing to go to any lengths to make sure the Asolo did not close. This time, however, general opinion was that people closest to the Asolo were at fault.

The problems had started with John Ulmer's contract being bought out in what some people considered to be an affront to both John and his supporters. His dismissal was followed by the selection of Margaret Booker, hailed as the leader the Asolo had never had who would take the company to the promised land. There was certainly abundant optimism in this change of direction; there were, however, important voices in the community that reacted with confusion and even anger. But those voices went unheeded. And unlike the '60s and '70s, when the Asolo was the only game in town, those patrons looking for a first-rate, community-oriented performing arts institution now had other choices.

Sarasota Magazine published two pieces in its November 1994 issue that looked back on the Asolo's recent history and attempted to diagnose what had happened. A feature by Porter Anderson found a new party at fault:

> *Maybe the Asolo should have been allowed to die in July. You think I'm writing heresy? Try this. The pious chorus from audience members, donors and the now-repentant and chastened board is that all the theater's sorrows came from aiming for national glory and turning its back on Sarasota, which had supported it for so many years. Did the Asolo "forget its community" as so many say it did? I don't think so. I think that the Old Asolo of Art turned into the New Asolo of the $16 million corporate headquarters, and the new Asolo (let's call it the First National Bank of Asolo) gave* in *to that community. Sarasota, because of its upscale demographics, became an extreme example of the gravest national mistake made by all the arts and especially theater—the alignment of art with wealth and social sophistication. If the company is to give the community the glitz it wants, or that it demanded in the hubris-crazed '80s, rather than the art it deserves, then what's been saved here? I guess Bob Strane understood long before the rest of us at Asolo that expensive architecture and opening night glamour aren't enough to keep 'em in the seats once the lights go out.*

It was Pam Daniel, editor of *Sarasota Magazine*, who had invited Anderson to give his take on the Asolo's problems. She knew he had a way of "ruffling feathers" and that his outspoken and acerbic reviews often offended. So, as she wrote in her column, she expected something provocative:

> *But I didn't expect his article to provoke* me, *or to leave me feeling as uneasy and defensive as it did when I first read it. The problem wasn't that the Asolo forgot what Sarasota wanted. The problem was that during the go-go '80s, the Asolo gave us exactly what the community* asked *for—a grand and glittering edifice that lacked nothing but an artistic soul. Suddenly, art becomes the "product" that must keep the grand new structure afloat rather than the heart and soul that keep it alive. Many of Sarasota's arts institutions have managed to stay vital as they grow and expand—the Florida West Coast Symphony and Florida Studio Theatre come immediately to mind. Look at the Sarasota Opera, which probably attracts more beaded gowns and fur wraps per seat than any other show in town, but which consistently presents top-quality productions. The challenge for all of us who create art—from plays to publications—for this demanding community is not to resist growth, but to keep our eyes on the ball. We need writing that inspires and speaks to the heart as well as splashy advertising and fancy paper, characters that stir our souls along with brilliant lighting*

> *and pretty costumes; and moments that enlarge our understanding more than moments that leave us empty and untouched.*

Had the Asolo, as Bob Strane once feared, become "an elitist toy, the darling of some set"?

The financial situation was approaching meltdown. In early spring of 1994, the staff and remaining board members met in search of working capital that would keep the company alive. Just as it seemed that the theatre would have to close its doors, board member Steve Smith came up with a proposal that would prevent the worst from happening—at least for the immediate future.

Some time before this crisis, donors had raised $240,000 that was then deposited in the state of Florida's Fine Arts Endowment Fund. The state added $120,000, creating a $360,000 endowment for the theatre. In a contractual agreement with the donors and the state, only the interest from the $360,000 could be used by the Asolo. Smith argued that rather than let the Asolo close, the endowment should be invaded. The plan was ultimately approved. The $240,000 could now be used as working capital, and the state was promptly refunded its $120,000. This, while keeping the theatre alive for the next few months, did not balance the books; there were still debts to be paid.

Shortly afterward, and despite bleak prospects for the future, Linda DiGabriele, literary manager Bruce Rodgers and conservatory head Brant Pope tried to move forward by choosing a 1994–95 season for both theatres (the Mertz and the conservatory's adjacent Cook Theatre, which would be ready to open by the season's start in the fall of 1994). "I think we strayed from our own community, and we weren't listening hard enough," Linda said. "We're now making a lot of attempts to reach out to the community…and we've selected a season for next year that we feel reflects the style so successful in our 34-year history." The plays included *Arms and the Man* and *The Glass Menagerie* in the Mertz and *The Winter's Tale* and *Broadway Bound* in the Cook.

The Bette Oliver Theatre in the Frankel Building had plain cinderblock walls, recycled seats and air conditioning that did not always work, but its acoustics, sightlines and stripped-down charm made it a fine performance space. It had seen many memorable productions. Now that the Cook Theatre was almost ready to open, the Bette Oliver would no longer be used.

In June, rumors began to circulate that the FSU Film Conservatory would be moving back to Tallahassee by the fall of 1995. There was sad speculation as to what would happen to this new Asolo Center if both the Asolo company and the film conservatory were no longer occupants.

A fundraising drive that began in April 1994 aimed to raise $500,000 to cover the Asolo's future operating expenses. The community, though cautious of the Asolo's potential financial pitfalls, nevertheless poured forth contributions. Stuart Barger, now the president-elect of the board of directors, published a letter attempting to clarify the Asolo's predicament:

> *On July 1, the Asolo Center for the Performing Arts will arrive at the most critical point in its 34-year history. On that date, the board of directors will meet to determine whether the Asolo Theatre Company can continue or must close, based on the success of the current fundraising campaign, which began April 1 with two goals:*
>
> *1. To raise $500,000 in cash and escrowed funds by June 30 to cover operation expenses and carry the institution through Oct. 1, at which time revenue from next season's single-ticket sales will be available.*
>
> *2. To raise an additional $1.8 million in funds by December 1995 to retire all current debts and repay borrowing from endowment funds. This goal must be realized for the Asolo to attain long-term financial stability.*
>
> *Following the public announcement of the current financial crisis at the Asolo, the community has responded both with financial contributions and serious questions about the ability of the Asolo to reach financial stability and to produce an artistic product which merits continues community support. The purpose of this article is to respond to those questions.*
>
> *What Has the Asolo Done to Date to Cut Expenses and Achieve Financial Stability?*
>
> *During the past year, the Asolo has undergone extensive financial review to prepare a plan to achieve financial stability. The annual budget was cut from $4,921,989 for 1993-'94 to $2,900,000 for 1994-'95. The staff has been reduced from 37 full-time and 23 season people to 19 full-time and 18 seasonal people.*
>
> *What Is Happening to the Relationship between the Asolo, Florida State University and the FSU/Asolo Conservatory?*
>
> *Florida State University and the Asolo have reached agreement where FSU will provide $400,000 annually in salaries for six non-tenured, renewable faculty positions at the Asolo Theatre.*

WHY DOESN'T ASOLO SIMPLY CLOSE ITS DOORS, GO "DARK" OR "BANKRUPT," RELIEVE ITSELF OF ALL DEBT AND REOPEN AS THE "NEW ASOLO"?

Many in the community have expressed a willingness to close the institution. That is not an alternative which is acceptable to the board. Closure will come only as a last resort. This would be an extreme disservice to local banks that have provided support through their loans, to local businesses that have accounts payable from the Asolo and to local members of the community who have personally guaranteed substantial amounts of the Asolo debt. It's our estimate that to restart the Asolo Theatre Company after any period of being "dark" would require a cash investment of over $2 million. [Those closest to the crisis were certain that if the Asolo closed it would never reopen, and there was doubt that a professional theatre would ever again occupy the Performing Arts Center. Stuart Barger was at times the one voice protesting against declaring bankruptcy or simply closing the doors.]

HOW CAN I BE ASSURED THAT THE ASOLO WILL SURVIVE IF I GIVE MONEY OR BUY SUBSCRIPTIONS?

We are offering no guarantees, only the assurance that the current board of directors is making every effort to restructure the organization to achieve financial stability and to produce theatre that will meet the expectations of the local community. Should we fail, we would appeal to fellow arts organizations to assist us in finding ways to honor our subscribers' investments.

And then there were the letters—letters from the veteran actors and directors who were most responsible for the high-quality work in the 1960s and '70s that gained widespread praise for the Asolo and bound it to the community. These members of the Asolo's history shared their passion for the institution:

Polly Holliday:

> *It was my training and experience at the Asolo Theatre from 1962–72 that made me confident and able to have a 30-year career as an actor. I am forever grateful to have had the Asolo as my "acting home" where I was given the time to practice and absorb great plays and roles. Sarasota has been blessed with live* real *theatre for many years and I have always been thankful for its existence and the part I was allowed to plays in it.*

David S. Howard:

I am extremely grateful to have been a member of the Asolo family. The company was a magnet for theatre people from all parts of the country. It was "Sarasota's own," and yet it had a national reputation for excellence. Now the Asolo has a new home, a different kind of schedule, perhaps a new audience, but the jewel can still shine, in a new and hopefully brighter way. Please keep it glowing.

Stephen Johnson:

The Asolo Repertory's production history stands as a tribute to its artists and craftspeople, and its ongoing influence is inestimable. It is part of the essential linkage between the classical tradition and the current mainstream.

Sharon Spelman:

I spent three years at the Asolo. That was 25 years ago, and I have yet to find another working experience that fulfilling. The bonds we formed then flourish today. We were a vital part of the community. Those years at the Asolo are among the brightest lights in my memory.

Michael Keenan:

It would be more than a shame, it would be a crime to lose an institution that has been seminal and nurturing to so many of the theatre artists who now populate the big and small screen and national stage. The Asolo is a part of this century's heritage to be preserved not as a relic, but as the provider of spoken art for a community and the training for the young.

William Leach:

The Asolo nurtured me when I needed it. She gave me discipline when I needed it. She seasoned me through six years of work as an actor. Furthermore, these artists who devoted their lives and talents to making the Asolo truly unique make up its history of excellence. A value of excellence I carry with me always.

Howard Millman:

In 1968 the Sarasota community banded together to save the Asolo Theatre. I am confident that the spirit and commitment then exhibited is still there.

Walter Rhodes:

I trust that Sarasotans, Floridians and loyal supporters everywhere will unite to address the present needs of the Asolo, restore its once clear vision, and set it on its dynamic course again. That this great theatre's mission should not continue, all of us know, is unacceptable.

Robert Strane:

As a founding director of Asolo, and a member of its company for 21 years, I need hardly to say how I feel about its present crisis. The threat of closing its doors represents to me an incalculable loss. More than a place of amusement, the Asolo is a beacon of Sarasota's cultural life and a monument to the many who have given so generously, not only of their wealth, but of themselves. So while I recognize that the financial climate for the arts has changed along with the rest of the economy, I urge my fellow Sarasotans to consider whether they cannot afford not *to support the recovery of so valuable a treasure.*

Eberle Thomas and Barbara Redmond:

When we say "Save the Asolo," we do so not for the sake of its illustrious past but for its potentially brilliant future. No organization can literally return to its roots. But this one has the chance to address itself anew to the simple but demanding goal set by Richard Fallon in the 1960s: To develop a first-rate ensemble of theatre artists dedicated to serving the citizens of Sarasota and the larger community of Florida. The theatre is one of the last places we can go to hear the truth. The Asolo is a treasure too precious to cast away.

Isa Thomas:

For 27 years, the Asolo was in a very deep sense my home. Emotionally and artistically it still is my home. Together as a daring and joyful collaboration

> *with our audience (the community), we took bold chances and grew as artists and as human beings. The true loss we are suffering now is the loss of this collaboration. If the doors of the Asolo are closed, the message will read: "You can't go home again; you cannot recover the trust—the dream." We ask for the chance to try.*

For our part, Marian and I submitted the following:

> *During our years here, we have seen the Asolo introduce thousands of Florida's young people to the wonders of live theatre, provide a professional environment to one of the finest conservatories in the country and be an irreplaceable source of joy and enrichment to this community. Its mistakes can be corrected; its loss would be devastating.*

Privately, though I'd been freelancing successfully both locally and throughout the country, without Marian's position at the Asolo, our family would more than likely have to relocate.

On the Monday that began the last week in June 1994, it was announced that the Selby Foundation was pledging a "capping grant" of $100,000. The grant would be awarded if the remaining money could be raised. If not, at five o'clock that coming Friday, the Asolo Theatre would go out of business. Friday afternoon, staff members gathered outside Linda DiGabriele's third-floor office to find out if the Asolo would survive.

Finally, the headlines reflected a change of fortune: "ASOLO THEATRE RESCUED IN TIME," "LAST-MINUTE CASH PRESERVES ASOLO," "FALL SHOWS WILL GO ON AT ASOLO," "ASOLO STAYS ALIVE WITH LAST-MINUTE DONATION."

During that final week in June, donations had flooded the Asolo's account at NationsBank. They ranged from $20 to the $100,000 grant from the Selby Foundation. Asolo board members contributed $213,000, NationsBank Community Foundation gave $50,000 and there were two anonymous $50,000 donations. Twenty thousand dollars came from a Los Angeles theatrical producer, $10,000 from RISCORP and $15,000 from the Tampa Bay Buccaneers (Gay Culverhouse, daughter of team owner Hugh Culverhouse, was on the Asolo board). But by Thursday afternoon, as the clock ran down, the goal still had not been reached. Longtime Asolo employee Donna Gerdes, then the business manager, took it upon herself to go to Esther Mertz and apprise her of the situation. At four o'clock on Thursday afternoon, Esther Mertz, the Asolo's guardian angel, wrote a check for $75,000.

"That's when we knew we were going over the top," said Steve Smith. One employee described the last forty-eight hours as "nail-biting time. We really weren't sure if we were going to have jobs next week."

The theatre would not close, announced board chairman John Welch (who had with his wife, Myrna, been prepared to mortgage their house to save the Asolo), but the community was demanding a shakeup in the board to try and guarantee that those past mistakes would not be repeated. "We need more businesspeople," he said, "people who know how to handle money."

And there were more reasons to be optimistic about the future. After the fundraising triumph that saved the company, the state's division of cultural affairs had audited the Asolo's financial situation and decided things were stable enough now to grant $291,000 per year to the Asolo for the next three years. Because of the cuts that had been made (including a 54 percent decrease in full-time staff and a 32 percent reduction in production budget), the theatre could save more than $400,000 over the next five years.

It should be emphasized that during this most critical period, the Asolo never bounced a check.

Toward the end of October 1994, Donna Gerdes, now the Asolo's acting executive director, announced that the Asolo Center for the Performing Arts was preparing to file suit against Burt Reynolds for failure to make payments on his $1 million pledge. Reynolds owed the Asolo a total of $795,000 and had not made a payment of $75,000 that was due in 1994. "He made the pledge in writing," Donna said. "It is definitely enforceable."

As noted before, Reynolds had experienced problems with his health that prevented him from working. He was now $11.8 million in debt and had a negative net worth of $2.56 million.

His fans were up in arms that a regional theatre dare sue a megastar. In a letter to the editor, Stuart Barger tried to explain: "It is absolutely essential that the funds pledged during a capital campaign be reached. Failure to do so can jeopardize matching and capping grants, prevent the organization from reaching its anticipated goal or, worst of all, find the organization in the middle of its activities without sufficient funds to continue. Failure to fulfill a pledge can be more damaging to an organization than failure to give at all." It was also noted that Reynolds's pledge in 1984 was the basis for the drive that would fund the new building.

Florida State University emphasized that it had no part of the lawsuit brought against one of its most generous supporters. In a statement issued by FSU president Sandy D'Alemberte, he explained:

> *The Asolo Theatre Inc. in Sarasota is independent of this university, even though we have many areas of common interest. Fiscal decisions are made by the Asolo Theatre Board of Directors, and I regret that their legal action involves Mr. Reynolds. In general, the university is concerned with the programmatic aspects of the Asolo Theatre operation. We are sad about this, because Mr. Reynolds has done so much for Florida State.*

The university stopped short of pressing the Asolo to drop the suit.

In June 1995, the suit's deadline expired. "Asolo officials said Thursday they were unable to serve Reynolds with a $770,000 lawsuit before an extended deadline for services expired this week," read an article in the *Herald-Tribune*. "The theater doesn't plan to go to court seeking a second extension of the deadline, although it may re-file the suit which seeks the unpaid portion of a $1 million pledge that Reynolds made to the Asolo in the mid-1980s." The suit was never re-filed.

The new Cook Theatre, just feet from the grand Scottish opera house of the Mertz, is a simple, comfortable structure that focuses the audience's attention on the actors. It is an intimate space with 161 seats in eleven rows and the back row is less than forty feet from the edge of the stage. Because supporters had such affection for the conservatory students, it was hoped that having both theatres in one building might lessen the reservations that many patrons still had about the Asolo's future. The Cook opened its first production, Noel Coward's *Hay Fever*, on November 17, to good reviews.

I had the good fortune to play David Bliss in that production. Brant Pope directed.

Chapter 14

An Old/New Boss with Old/New Problems

I never really left.
—Howard Millman

After his tenure at the Asolo in the '70s, Howard Millman spent thirteen successful years as producing artistic director of the GeVa Theatre in Rochester, New York. He had raised annual subscription sales from three thousand to thirteen thousand and had overseen the theatre's move into the historic Rochester Armory. However, as sometimes happens in regional theatre, complaints arose about his choice of plays—that they were not "challenging" enough. Also, GeVa's new play festival had had to be cancelled because of a deficit of almost $1 million. And, possibly most important, Howard was becoming restless and had begun to look for a change. When I called and asked, informally, if he would be interested in returning to the Asolo, he said yes. Asked if his interest could be made known to key people in Sarasota, he said yes. He was one of 108 applicants for the Asolo job; the board and the FSU president unanimously approved his hire in February 1995. The position he would take, producing artistic director, was a new one for the Asolo, combining the duties of both artistic and executive directors.

Marian and I hosted one of Howard's "Welcome Home" parties.

I was not the only person to feel that there was perhaps no person in the country, other than Howard Millman, who had a chance of putting the Asolo back on its feet. A new and unknown director would have required a "honeymoon," a wait-and-see first season for the public to assess the choice of plays, the quality of the productions, ticket sales and the director's relationship with the community. After the Margaret Booker debacle, patience had worn thin. Supporters remembered Howard for his part in creating a hugely successful Asolo during the Soaring '70s and personally respected and liked him for his politician's confidence. Michael Millard, GeVa's chairman, sent him off to Sarasota saying, "He brings great experience and a tremendous sense of energy with him. You guys are lucky to have him."

Howard said of his decision to return, "I never really left. Probably the strongest ties of friendship in my life were formed at the Asolo. There's a whole network of people who were there when I was, who shared the same triumphs and agonies. This bound us together in a spiritual sort of way."

Understanding recent resentment and anger, Howard asked that Asolo supporters put their focus on the future. He said the Asolo had to "take a stand on what it is and where it's going. Part of the problem is that people don't know what we stand for."

He vowed a return to the classics—not only the likes of Shakespeare and Shaw but also works by modern masters such as O'Neill and Tennessee Williams. He pointedly recalled that during his first tenure, the Asolo had produced such contemporary writers as Tom Stoppard, John Guare and Harold Pinter, as well as producing new plays within the repertory. He aimed to once again create a balanced repertoire.

Essential to the Asolo's future was the reinstatement of a system of rotating repertory. Having three or more plays rotating performances from day to day had always been ideal for a city that drew vacationers for several days or longer. In an interview with the *Orlando Sentinel*, Howard explained:

> *Q. Why do we want to go back to rep?*
>
> *A. This is not going "back" to anything. It is an assertion of the artistic values that constitute the identity of the Asolo. Adoption of the rep system is a statement that we believe in certain things: in good action springing from an ensemble that only a company can create, in a commitment to place the great classics of dramatic literature at the heart of our work and stage them in a way made affordable only by rotating rep; by placing our primary efforts into giving the region what serves it best and maximizing the reality of highly seasonal audience and finally to take best advantage of the presence of a professional training conservatory and incorporating it into the artistic vision.*
>
> *Q. But we can't get good actors to commit to the rep, they don't want to leave the city for that long.*

A. Under this assumption, we have operated with stock runs during the past three years. Can anyone claim that we have been attracting great acting talent to the Asolo? On the contrary, the acting in the past three years has been very poor and should serve as proof that we have been seeking the wrong kind of background and commitment.

Q. Can we afford to do rotating rep?

A. We can't afford not to. Here are some of the reasons why rotating rep offers unequaled financial opportunities:
a. Victor Meyrich has stated that rep is actually cheaper to run than a stock season. He can document why this is true. We have an incredible source in Victor in that he has established an efficient way of making the rep work.
b. The design and production costs will be lower; designers can be contracted to create more than one design, thus eliminating the continual need to hire and transport a whole design team per show.
c. The actor costs can be decreased: 16–20 actors per season can be hired instead of forty-plus.
d. The conservatory can be fully incorporated and utilized in ways that have substantial benefits. Conservatory actors become part of the company and the opportunity to really use the conservatory as a young company reduces the need to hire 25–35 year old actors to play these roles.

"The relationship that develops between the company and the community can be wonderful," Howard said of the necessity for a resident company. "People look forward to seeing actors they recognize do different roles, and display their range. The actors become part of the community, and a sense of trust develops. The theatre is allowed to take chances, and even fail once in a while." And to reinforce his point, he planned to bring back familiar faces from the past, as well as a very special support organization.

Donna Gerdes told me:

The Asolo Theatre Festival Association served its purpose when we were still a small organization, but as we grew the fundraising activities were then taken over by the Asolo's development department, which it never had before. The Angels still existed, but from 1989 to 1995 did not have any officers nor did they meet. In 1995, through the board's efforts, it was thought to be a good fundraising move to once again organize the Angels to make them feel more a part of the new building, the new theatre and the new management.

Howard became an associate director of the Asolo/FSU Conservatory, too, and with the Cook Theatre adjacent to the Mertz in the same building, the tie between the two could be reinforced. Howard and Brant Pope, who in addition to his conservatory role was also the Asolo's associate artistic director at the time, now announced their separate seasons in the same brochure. For the 1995–96 season, the mainstage would open with a straight run of a musical version of *Jane Eyre*. The repertory would follow with former associate director Eb Thomas's adaptation of *The Three Musketeers* and would include *The Taming of the Shrew* and *Look Homeward, Angel.*

The second-year students' season in the Cook would include David Mamet's *American Buffalo* and Chekov's *Uncle Vanya.* The community that had so generously and lovingly supported the conservatory was gratified to know that, thanks to Howard, third-year students would now be doing major roles in mainstage productions. During the first two years, the students took classes and had their own season in the Cook; as for the third-year students, Howard said, "They're mine."

The first-year students once again understudied actors for the mainstage productions. In 1980, Dan Haughey, then a second-year student in the conservatory, wrote a paper in which he described his experience as an

Kris Danford and SaRa Schabach in the FSU-Asolo Conservatory production of *Mirandolina* by Carlo Goldoni.

understudy: "The system serves the student-actor as an effective 'learning tool' on two levels. As an artist, the understudy is provided a practical means by which to gain the necessary knowledge to create the role. As a student, the understudy is provided a practical means by which to study his craft."

Meanwhile, the Asolo board was undergoing a significant change in its makeup. Several longtime members had resigned. Of the four new members, three were from Manatee County. The new board president, Don Roberts, explained, "We're looking for a balance between Sarasota and Manatee. From now on, we'll be rotating the presidency between the counties." (Though long considered a Sarasota institution, both Asolo Theatres were located on the border between Sarasota and Manatee Counties.)

Howard's choice for the final show of the 1994–95 season was *Beehive*, a "rollicking '60s musical." Shaw's *Arms and the Man* had been a tremendous success during the interim year, but *Beehive* was to do even better, with box office receipts approaching $200,000. Success was breeding success. Subscription sales for the 1995–96 season were $700,000 over the same time the past year, and single ticket sales were keeping pace. "We've sold $19,000 in single ticket sales for *Jane Eyre* alone," Howard said. "Last year at this time we'd only sold $13,000 single tickets for all the plays in the season."

"Theater in this part of the world has to be much more than local, but it has to have local appeal to survive," said an editorial in the *Bradenton Herald*. "But it also has to generate a generous share of theatrical magic. Give us magic, Howard Millman, give us magic—and we'll follow you wherever you want to go."

During the spring of 1995, both Charlie Reimer and Arthur Dorlag passed away. Their conversation in 1959 marked the genesis of the Asolo Festival, and the debt that is owed to them is not often fully recognized.

Chapter 15

Not Yet Out of the Woods

We're on life support.
—*Howard Millman*

But around the time of Howard's hire, a newspaper article quietly revealed a dizzy canary in the theatre's coal mine. Florida's tourism industry saw a decline for the first time in three years. Commercialism, crowding and competition from other parts of the country were taking a toll. "Essentially, you've got a pie of a certain size and now you have more players that want to take a chunk out of it," said Florida Commerce Department spokesman Jim McClellan. Rampant publicity surrounding recent killings of foreign tourists didn't help.

In April 1995, even as ticket sales swelled and the box office reported sales ahead of the previous year, $525,000 in donations was still needed to ensure that the following season would occur at all. In fact, revenue for the previous season had been $145,000 below projections. The *Herald-Tribune* reported, "The Asolo—already carrying a $1.8 million debt load—will end its fiscal year on June 30 with a deficit of about $250,000, and will be forced to use some of next year's subscription money to pay current bills."

That summer, FSU moved its film conservatory from Sarasota to Tallahassee, citing financial reasons.

Howard admitted, "We have a severe cash-flow problem now, because we're incurring a lot of expenses getting the season going." Of the more than $1 million debt, he said, "I don't think we can make any dents in it until we get everything else in order." There was not enough money to make the payroll—frighteningly reminiscent of what we'd been told before the 1968 Educational Enrichment Tour hit the road.

This most recent financial muddle was not easily explained. Everything seemed rosy when Esther Mertz resolved the last fundraising drive that ended on June 30, 1994, followed by Howard Millman's return. Now, for some reason, the theatre stood on the brink of closing yet again. Howard, in an attempt to explain, contributed an article to local newspapers. He wrote:

> *When the Asolo had a problem two years ago, the $500,000 cash reserve it needed to raise was in addition to its normal $800,000 annual fundraising needs. The theatre had traditionally raised that amount in the past. When the community gave the additional amount, many people felt they had given their annual gift. Therefore, the theatre's annual fundraising needs were not met. In essence, we were right back in the same problem. I inherited the situation and can't help what has happened in the past; I can only try to lead this theatre forward to a new and hopefully prosperous future.*

Right now, he went on, "We're on life support."

Unfortunately, some potential donors in the community considered the Asolo bloated, inefficient and elitist. John Ulmer attempted to explain these feelings in an article he wrote for the *Sarasota Arts Review*:

> *Successful, generous, cultured members of a community who are motivated to help that community, gravitate, quite understandably, to the boards of local arts organizations. Few local symphonies, operas or theatres could operate without such fine, giving people to support them. Oddly, however, after a time, many of these same folk undergo a metamorphosis, abandoning their previous love of theatre as meaningful entertainment. They start to move their organizations toward some ill-defined lofty level of "art and beauty" tailored for the cognoscenti or a New York critic, should he be enticed to write about it. They hope to free their organizations from the bounds of local concerns and have it produce universal art which, along with a very expensive new building, will serve as a memorial to their time on the board.*

The Asolo needed another $500,000 for a reserve fund to see it through cash-poor periods—in addition to what was now a $1.2 million fund for the regular seasonal expenses. (The season ended, as before, at the end of the fiscal year on June 30.)

As of now, the theatre would be able to stay open until January 21, 1996. "Some have urged the Asolo to declare bankruptcy, get out from under its $1 million debt and start over," Howard said. "But it's not the debt that's killing us! We're making our debt payments. It's the cash-flow problems that are hurting us."

In mid-December, a worst-case scenario was made public: the board of directors had just contributed only enough to cover the next week's payroll, about $39,000. A shortfall loomed at the end of the month. "If money is not available," said Howard, "the company will be disbanded and the theatre will have to close."

When the Film Conservatory moved back to Tallahassee during the summer, it left the west side of the Asolo Center empty. The soundstage was now a rehearsal hall where full sets could be brought in and used for rehearsals. It was just before Christmas 1995, during a run-through of Michael Frayn's *Noises Off*, that a grim-faced Howard Millman, Linda DiGabriele and Bruce Rodgers entered the soundstage and told the company that the Asolo could close in January. For the actors, who had been so up and optimistic, this was a sudden and severe blow.

Once again, local editorials pleaded the Asolo's case:

The *Bradenton Herald*:

> *The Asolo Center for the Performing Arts cannot close. That ought to be the thought of every public official and every lover of the arts in Manatee and Sarasota counties—their mantra, their obsession, their bottom line. The Asolo Theatre cannot close.*

The *Longboat Observer*:

> *We feel badly for Howard Millman. When he returned recently to pick up the pieces and rebuild the Asolo, he encountered what easily could be considered an insurmountable task. But like all entrepreneurs, Millman is a believer. He is convinced in his gut, his heart and his mind that the Asolo can be saved and flourish—if only given the time and money. For decades the Asolo has been one of Sarasota's most prized assets. Much of what greater Sarasota is today—the arts capital of Florida—can be attributed to the Asolo.*

The *Sarasota Herald-Tribune*:

> *What the Asolo needs is time. Time to let the drama unfold, at a realistic pace, toward the rosier scenario that the supporters see in sight. They are looking for angels to believe in the Asolo, once more, for just a little longer. We hope they find them, waiting in the wings, enjoying the show thus far and ready to help.*

Indeed, what the Asolo needed was time.

Since the beginning of the year, actors had volunteered after curtain calls to try to explain the Asolo's problems and ask for help from the audience. Donations came from far and wide—including three dollars in allowance money from Gabe Piser, a ten-year-old boy from Pennsylvania.

Still, a similar cry for help had gone out less than two years before, and potential supporters demanded, *How do we know this won't happen again?* The Asolo management responded: "Two years ago the Asolo was rudderless, still reeling from the management of former artistic director Margaret Booker and executive director Lee Warner. Now a new leader, Howard Millman, is in charge, the theatre's board has been reconstituted, and the theatre has returned to its roots as a company that specializes in classic works performed in rotating repertory. For the first time in years, the box-office revenue is increasing." The aim, on every level, was to convince the public that the Asolo had seen the folly of its ways and was charting a new course.

Many Asolo patrons continued their strong support. "An empty theater is a mournful place," wrote board member Len Gumley in a letter to the editor. "If you have resentment of the past and/or questions about future of the Asolo, please call 351-9010, and we will attempt to answer all your questions. We want to reassure you that the Asolo is your theater and if you give us the opportunity, we will make you proud of it once again." Stuart Kaminsky, the former head of the FSU/Asolo Film Conservatory, felt that saving the Asolo was in the public interest. "It is in the interest of government, business and industry to give the new Asolo the financial support it needs to overcome the past and to move quickly under its new management to solvency and quality," Kaminsky wrote. "The need for outside support beyond ticket sales will always exist, as it does for all regional and small theaters. Business, industry, banks, public: Respond immediately; or it will be too late and we will long regret it."

By mid-January, time was running out. In desperation, Asolo management brought together a small group of business and foundation executives and informed them that, without their financial support, the Asolo would have to close as early as the following week.

"We said that a Band-Aid solution wouldn't work, that the Asolo problem had to be fixed," Howard said. "They listened, and asked some pointed questions. They'll get back to us early next week."

The group insisted on budget cuts before any consideration could be given to donations. Even then, it might not be enough. "I think everyone was sympathetic," said Robert Perkins, executive director of the Selby Foundation, "but how that's going to translate into dollars, I'm not sure. Time restraints may make it difficult for some people to act quickly enough. And I don't know whether this coalition is big enough to do the job. Even if there's the will to help, I don't know if there's the capacity to help." On January 31, 1996, the Asolo had $258,000 in the bank, enough to keep it going until February 9.

But earlier in January, Howard Millman had received a telephone call from board member Roy Palmer. Palmer relayed an idea that would become yet another stroke of good fortune for a theatre that always seemed to be in the hands of Providence.

The Sarasota Ballet was about to break ground for a $2.3 million rehearsal/administrative complex to be built on city property near the Van Wezel Performing Arts Hall, just north of downtown Sarasota. There were rumors that the ballet was having trouble raising money and that they'd begun looking for an alternate plan. A ballet official contacted Roy Palmer and suggested a plan that would, in time, send shock waves through the arts community.

The ballet was prepared to give up plans to build its new home and move instead into the vacated west wing of the Asolo Center. The soundstage would become dance studios and the administrative offices, costume shop and education programs would be housed in the office and storage space. Officials on both sides stressed that the two organizations were not planning to merge.

In return, the ballet would hand over $1 million to FSU, and a significant portion of that would, in turn, be given to the Asolo. "This is an alliance which everyone benefits from," said Dick Angelotti, chairman of the ballet's capital campaign. The Asolo could finish its 1995–96 season and establish a cash reserve fund. The ballet would invest $500,000 on renovations in its new facility but would still save about $750,000 by not constructing a whole new building—and the organization would have better parking and ten thousand more square feet of rehearsal space than originally planned, as well as access to the Mertz stage for performances. Supporters of the arts, in turn, would endure fewer requests to fund building projects and their associated operation expenses.

"If all the pieces come together, this will make the Asolo debt-free and on sound financial footing," said Dick Olson, vice-president of the Asolo board. The businesses and foundations the Asolo had pleaded with in January would be more inclined to pay off the $750,000 owed to Florida lenders, and FSU might forgive the Asolo's $900,000 debt. Howard, board members Roy Palmer and Dick Angelotti and the ballet's director, Robert DeWarren, were given credit for putting the plan together. And amazingly enough, through all this preparation, no word was leaked to the public.

"Brilliant! A stroke of genius," said the *Bradenton Herald.* "The payoff is that it will provide local residents the fine artistic product they deserve with a price tag they can afford." This preliminary arrangement had been put together in less than three weeks. In July 1996, the agreement was finalized. "You can't imagine the bureaucratic morass we've had to fight our way through to marry the Asolo and the ballet and FSU," said Roy Palmer. "But I've never seen such cooperation."

The new stability attracted an infusion of high-profile Asolo board members. Stanley Kane, a major leader in the Sarasota arts community, became the board's president and was using his influence to make sure the Asolo did not stumble again. "Stanley has called in all his chips," one board member said. "He's convinced people that the Asolo is worth saving and that they should be involved." Kane added, "I'm putting my money where my mouth is, and I'm confident that others will, too."

Jean Weidner, the founder of the Sarasota Ballet and a keen fundraiser, also became an Asolo board member. "My main interest is in what's best for the community, and the Asolo is obviously a major asset," she said. "I believe strongly in synergy between organizations, and I'm eager to be involved. I sense that everybody is pumped up and there's a great deal of excitement. We're not going to fail."

With the Asolo and the ballet together in the same building, the complex's name needed to be reconsidered. It was proposed that what was then the Asolo Center for the Performing Arts should be changed to the Florida State University Center for the Performing Arts. The university, after all, owned the building and had played a role in bringing the Asolo and the ballet together. Of course, a hue and cry arose at the prospect of the Asolo name losing its featured place on the granite marker out front. "Some people in Sarasota feel strongly about the tradition of the Asolo name," said Gil Lazier. "And they're concerned about any change." The ballet, on the other hand, felt the change would be appropriate, so as not to feel "like guests in an Asolo building." Still, for a time, Sarasota Ballet brochures bore the compromise, "FSU/Asolo Center," so that people could still identify the building. The official name change occurred in February 1997. The west wing, which contained the soundstage that had once been named for Burt Reynolds, was named for Marvin and Betty Danto, two of the ballet's generous supporters.

John Ulmer died in late June 1996. Many in the Sarasota arts community attended a memorial service for him at the Golden Apple Dinner Theatre on the first Sunday in July.

Chapter 16

The Gamble Pays Off

A new restoration effort is afoot on a now quiet stage.
—Phillip Hall

The Asolo company, now free from immediate financial threats, enjoyed renewed growth. The productions in the 1995–96 season were selling well, and the community sensed that the Asolo was back on the same track that had led to its early success.

Now everyone's knight in shining armor, Howard Millman suddenly seemed bent on hoisting himself on his own petard. The 1996–97 season would open with David Edgar's adaptation of Charles Dickens's novel, *Nicholas Nickleby*, which the playwright had titled *The Life and Adventures of Nicholas Nickleby, Parts I and II*. Directed by Eb Thomas and his wife, Barbara Redmond, each of the two parts was expected to run under four hours, including intermissions, and require a complex set, choreographic staging and actors performing multiple roles. *Why this dangerous choice*, people asked, *when the Asolo is now correcting the ruinous mistakes of the past?* (Local wags referred to the opening productions as *Howard's End*, a play on the title of the novel by E.M. Forster.) Would the Asolo return to the feast-or-famine seesaw that had, even recently, so disillusioned its supporters?

In early December, the production opened. "*Nicholas Nickeby* is live theater at its best," wrote Charlie Husking. "A compelling play crammed with poignant and funny moments, and performed by a stellar cast."

The *Bradenton Herald*:

> *As the Asolo Theatre Company opens its season, there should be a collective sigh of relief. Their masterful production of* The Life and Adventures of Nicholas Nickleby, Parts I and II, *is an absolute gem: Colorful, engaging, suitably moody and a pure delight.*

The *Venice Gondolier*:

> *The Asolo Theatre Company, and Howard Millman producing artistic director, has opened a monumental, memorable and mesmerizing production of the stage adaptation. This is an astounding theatrical achievement. With 26 performers playing 150 different characters, the mere act of efficiently and effectively moving them around the stage, as they have done, is quite an accomplishment: that they have done so with artistry and aplomb, displays a master's touch.*

The *Tampa Tribune*:

> *You won't often find a production of this magnitude, skill and richness.* Nicholas Nickleby *is far too big, complicated and difficult a show for 99.9 percent of this country's theater companies to put on. Be grateful that producing artistic director Howard J. Millman has revived the Asolo's resident ensemble. Be grateful that you again have a repertory company in your back yard. Then take the family—and the children who can sit three hours at a time—to the theater for a show you won't forget.*

Arguably the most eloquent review was a letter to the editor written by Lola F. Laubheim, a Sarasota resident and Asolo patron:

> *If Sarasota had no attractions other than the current production of* The Life and Adventures of Nicholas Nickleby, Parts I and II, *it would still be worth a visit from the most distant places. I have seen theater in all parts of the United States and in London, but the Asolo performance that I saw recently is equal to the best. The acting and ensemble work are notable; the direction is sensitive; the audience is drawn into the play before it begins as the characters mingle with the audience. Changes from humor to pathos and from pathos to humor are smooth and credible. The play is several hours long, but the audience is involved and no one appears to be*

> *restless. As I left the theater, I had an upsurge of feeling that it is wonderful to be alive, that goodness will prevail and that happy endings are possible. Charles Dickens would have been proud of the direction and production of this* Nicholas Nickleby *and, if it were possible, he would certainly make sure that he got to Sarasota to see this masterpiece performed by the talented actors and actresses at the Asolo. Anyone who wants to give himself an outstanding Christmas, birthday or un-birthday present should buy a ticket soon. When they hear of this in New York or California, it may be too late.*

The actors had always had faith that *Nickleby* was going to succeed—largely because of Eb Thomas's and Barbara Redmond's detailed direction, which was both a challenge and a treat for us.

The Asolo had turned a corner, and the monumental gamble had paid off. For the first time in over a decade, patrons, staff, actors and Asolo leadership enjoyed a sense of positive focus. The solid foundation that had been laid down during the formative years could now be rebuilt brick by brick. The success that began with *Nickleby* set a precedent for years to come.

"A Magnificent Turnaround," was the *Bradenton Herald*'s headline. "What a difference a year makes. This season the Asolo is playing to sold-out houses and warning patrons not to delay renewing their season subscriptions for next season or they might be disappointed."

Jonathan Robinson as Nicholas Nickleby in a stage adaptation by David Edgar. *Photo by Gary W. Sweetman.*

"I think *Nicholas* has more than accomplished the purpose I set out for," said Howard. "We had an audience to recover, we had an audience to retrain, to retell what we were, to recapture the great glory of the Asolo that we had—and *Nicholas* was able to accomplish that purpose."

In March 1997, the Asolo marketing department reported attendance was 69 percent of capacity, as opposed to 49 percent for the same period the season before. Subscriptions had grown from four thousand to six thousand, a 50 percent increase. Sales reached 66 percent of the overall season ticket goal with over 50 percent of performances remaining. The result was that the theatre had already earned 81 percent of the year's total anticipated ticket revenue.

John Barron, the manager of the Asolo's subscription campaign, had promised to dress as a cherub and run around the Asolo building if more than six thousand subscriptions were sold. The number was surpassed, and Barron made good on his pledge. The goal for the next season was set at eight thousand subscriptions.

It was Howard's intention to make the Asolo "the winter destination theatre of North America." And to that end, the Asolo had again set out to bolster its national image—not so much to impress New York critics as to draw a national audience to complement the regional supporters. The theatre now boasted a website, a visitors' guide, group sales brochures, an ad in *American Theatre* magazine and an article in *Variety*.

As the fiscal year came to a close, it was evident that the Asolo would finish the season with a balanced budget for the first time in the '90s. The Asolo was winning back the trust and affection of the region; corporate and individual donations had increased significantly. Donna Gerdes, now the Asolo's development director, set about building the Asolo endowment.

In 1995, a grant for $476,000 had been awarded to the city of Sarasota for the restoration of the Ringling Towers, a landmark hotel near downtown Sarasota. Because of technicalities having to do with ownership, however, the hotel was subsequently deemed ineligible. State Senator Katherine Harris (R—Sarasota) worked out an arrangement whereby the grant would be redirected to the Sarasota County Arts Council, which could then distribute the money to various arts groups in Sarasota. The Asolo received $100,000 in 1997. Dick Morris, a member of the Sarasota Film Society (which was not funded by the Cultural Institutions program), expressed frustration that money did not go back into the state's general operating fund. The Asolo's share was particularly upsetting, because, as he said, "The Asolo has been a rat hole for the misuse of state funds."

Other arts leaders—including Bill Mitchell of the Van Wezel Performing Arts Hall and John Jacobson of Florida Studio Theatre—praised Senator Harris for her contribution to the arts in Sarasota.

There had been a town meeting at the Mertz Theatre before the 1994 season, and, as a testament to the state of the Asolo dilemma at the time, only a handful of people showed up. In September 1997, patrons packed the

Mertz for the coming season's announcement, and each actor received his own ovation during introductions. It felt like home again.

During the 1997–98 season, a special actor joined the company—one Howard Millman, who was cast as Mervyn Kant in *The Sisters Rosensweig.* "The character is a still-somewhat sexy 58-year-old Jewish furrier from New York," Howard said. "I think I can handle that."

Sharon Spelman and Howard Millman in *The Sisters Rosensweig* by Wendy Wasserstein. *Photo by James Fry.*

After the season opened, Asolo publicist Holly Brown had to apologize because so many performances had so few good seats left. A "standby" ticket policy began whereby the best available sold but unclaimed seats could be had for twenty-five dollars. At this point, the goal of eight thousand subscriptions sold for the coming season was well within reach.

After sixteen years as dean of FSU's School of Theatre, Gil Lazier decided to step down in August 1998 in order to spend more time teaching. Besides having overseen the steady growth of the conservatory, Gil had also played an important part in efforts to save the Asolo. Furthermore, Jay Handleman wrote in the *Herald-Tribune*, "He created a program with the Moscow Art Theatre and FSU that allowed the exchange of 80 Russian and American students and 12 faculty members. He also established the London Theatre Experience, a semester of study with professional theatre artists and English professors that is required for Asolo Conservatory students at the end of their second year of study." (At this writing, the London trip remains a highlight of students' conservatory experiences.) He would eventually follow Brant Pope as conservatory head in 2002.

At a gala event, Bruce Rodgers, now the Asolo's associate artistic director, was given a special "Renaissance Leadership Award" by the Sarasota County Arts Council "for his work at the Asolo writing new plays (including *Lost Electra* and *The Gravity of Honey*) and for his leadership position allying schools with arts education."

In 1999, the theatre that had failed its community and friends, that nearly closed half a dozen times in its history, happily celebrated its fortieth anniversary. On February 6, the Chelsea Center in south Sarasota was packed with supporters and friends who celebrated the Asolo's miraculous recovery as a centerpiece of Sarasota's cultural life.

Barbara Rothstein, Asolo event chairman, staged a celebration that included searchlights, TV cameras and a beautifully decorated center. "Here we are celebrating not only our history," Howard said, "but our stamina, our ability to overcome adversity, and above all our artistry. We here are the beneficiaries of a great vision, the very best in theatre." Following his remarks, Howard, Eb Thomas and I guided the audience through a slideshow that highlighted the Asolo's history. The evening's emotional high point occurred when Dick Fallon embraced Howard, who had been Dick's student at FSU nearly fifty years before, and praised him for bringing the Asolo back from the brink of bankruptcy.

Robert Strane died in early May 2000 after a long battle with cancer. Within a few days, old Asolonians gathered on the mezzanine lobby of the Asolo Center. Friends and colleagues shared stories about Bob and his place in the Asolo's history. Vic Meyrich, who had clashed with Bob over the years, said that if he were to be stranded on a desert island with people of his own choosing, he would want Bob Strane to be one of them. Bob, a brilliant, passionate and, yes, temperamental man, had that effect on people. Unable to attend, Dick Fallon sent a letter in which he called Bob "the pillar of the golden age of the Asolo." We gave witness to his monumental importance in taking a new venture and building something that would last for years to come. Refreshments were beer and pizza—an appropriate ode, I thought, to the life of Dr. Robert Strane, a man so proud of his impersonation of Little Richard.

Bob's passing inspired a new movement in Sarasota regarding the historic Asolo, the original little theatre from Italy. The theatre had not been used

Burton Clark as the fool and Robert Strane as Shakespeare's King Lear. *Photo by Gary W. Sweetman.*

for play productions in more than ten years, and Laurence Rugerio, the Ringling Museum's director during that time, had not made its upkeep a top priority. What had once been the exquisite jewel box was now a shabby shadow of its former self. Seats showed their age, there were water stains on the ceiling and immediately behind the drawn act curtain was a vault that had been built on stage to store artwork. The only usable space—had anyone cared to use it—was the narrow forestage.

"I would ask the citizens of Sarasota to honor the memory of Bob Strane by demanding that the Ringling Museum restore [the Asolo] to its former state," Dick Fallon wrote in a letter to the editor. "Once restored, have a tablet placed with the names of Bob Strane and all those who created this miracle of the Asolo Theatre Company."

Dick was seconded by Phillip Hall, the former executive director of the Sarasota Opera, who wrote:

> *I think it's fair to say that the theater and vocal arts in Sarasota would not have blossomed to the extent they have without the museum's Asolo theater.*

> *The recent demise of Robert Strane should, indeed, be the catalyst for the restoration of the Asolo—as a theater!...After a decade in the shadows, amid frequent mutterings from the community that a valued resource was being neglected, the Asolo is back in the spotlight. A new restoration effort is afoot on a now quiet stage.*

Florida State University assumed control of the Ringling Museum in the summer of 2000. In September, FSU president Sandy D'Alemberte requested a plan from the Asolo for a Sarasota cultural center that could include a variety of organizations and purposes. In keeping with the legacy of Chick Austin, education was a top priority. There should be classes for tourists and local seniors, families and children in theatre, art and dance. The initial plan was to be put together by Bruce Rodgers.

The Historic Asolo Theater, as would become its official name, was closed to the public in early February 2001 as restoration moved forward. John Wetenhall, the museum's new executive director, outlined a plan that included a new visitors' center, an expanded circus museum and more exhibition and educational space. The little theatre might find itself in yet another new home.

Renovation of the theatre alone was estimated at several million dollars and ten years to completion. The funding, however, could be expedited, because as a part of FSU, the museum was eligible for state matching grants. President D'Alemberte knew that the new visitors' center could be years away and felt the renovation of the theatre and its present home could be done more quickly and for less money. One way or the other, the theatre was to be restored.

Jody Peary, the Asolo's longtime ultra-competent executive secretary, died in February 2002. For decades, her delightful spirit had done so much for the company's morale.

In September, FSU trustees awarded $43 million for the museum's expansion. The final plan was assembled by Ringling board chairman Vern Buchanan and FSU officials, who had decided that the historic Asolo would be restored and reassembled in the new visitors' center. The funding would require local supporters to raise $10 million to cover the museum's operations, but leaders were optimistic that this would pose no problem. Bob and Linda Roskamp led the way with a $1 million donation.

Chapter 17

FSU Asolo: The Tempest

Together we will help each other as we continue the transition from the old system to the new guy.
—Dean Steven Wallace

And then began a series of the most bizarre episodes in the history of the Asolo.

Howard Millman had been expected to retire in of 2003 because he had signed up for a "voluntary enhanced retirement program" with FSU, which had been paying his salary along with five other Asolo employees: the managing director, the associate artistic director, the production manager, the director of costume design and the marketing director. In December 2002, Howard changed his mind, and the Asolo board agreed to pick up his salary. If that was to be the case, FSU said, then the university could not pay the other five salaries—the argument being that it couldn't have its employees answering to someone who was not on the FSU payroll. The five were notified that their contracts would be terminated in six months. The new FSU president, T.K. Wetherell, provost Larry Abele and dean of the school of theatre Steven Wallace became the university's chief spokesmen on the matter.

So far, FSU's action seemed reasonable. However, some Asolo board members feared the university was moving to influence the selection of the Asolo's next head man—thereby taking more control of the theatre. There was also a rumor that provost Larry Abele disliked Howard and the Asolo, but the university denied that either was the case. And so the Asolo found itself ushered into yet another convoluted situation.

On January 23, 2003, a *Sarasota Herald-Tribune* headline read, "FSU, Asolo End 42-year Relationship."

The FSU spokesmen announced that the FSU/Asolo Conservatory would be moved to Tallahassee, where the program would be headed by film and TV actress Jane Alexander. The announcement stunned the Sarasota community. Dean Wallace contended that the dispute with Howard ("The Asolo reversed directions on us.") was only one of several factors in the decision to move, but local opinion was that FSU was being spiteful after being denied the chance to have more control. The university countered that there were also major problems financing the program in Sarasota. It was noted that FSU had contributed more than $12 million in the recent past to keep the theatre alive.

In Tallahassee, acting students would be able to work with the graduate programs in directing, design and film. The present first-year class would be the last to graduate from the Sarasota campus, and no new students would be recruited until the program moved to Tallahassee. State Senator Lisa Carlton (R—Osprey) moved quickly and asked FSU to reconsider its decision.

"The tempest over Howard Millman is difficult to understand," said Asolo supporter Dr. Robert Rosenbluth. "Whatever motivations are at work, be they over control or funds or egos or petty personality conflicts, they are misguided and will result in a disastrous outcome for the Asolo."

Henry Polic, a graduate of FSU enjoying a successful acting career in Los Angeles, was at the time conducting a workshop for the conservatory. "I don't ever remember FSU being driven by power and ego, but that's what this smacks of," he said. "And it's the kind of secretive action you'd expect from a company like Enron, not a university." Third-year conservatory student Kim Blair felt that FSU's actions showed a "lack of respect for Gil Lazier, who has been so integral to the FSU theatre program" (a program, incredulous supporters argued, that had just been named by the *New York Times* as one of the nine best actor training programs in the United States).

Senator Carlton was hard at work trying to bring the two sides together. But now, if the conservatory were allowed to stay in Sarasota, FSU representatives said, the lease would have to be renegotiated. After FSU had purchased the performing arts center in 1997, the agreement had been that the Asolo would pay $1 per year for forty years to lease the building. The Asolo also paid $200,000 per year to support the conservatory students. "On the one hand," said Senator Carlton, "if FSU negotiated a bad lease, that's not the Asolo's fault. But if it is really that one-sided, perhaps each side can give. If we can open the lines of communication, get people to compromise,

I truly believe we can work out these problems." But poor communication would continue to foul the water for both sides.

Supporters in Sarasota scratched their heads and asked, *What do they want?* Esther Mertz promised to discontinue her considerable contributions to the conservatory if it moved. When FSU would not answer her letters of concern, she concluded, "They don't seem to be a group of gentlemen up there anymore."

The Asolo's $200,000 each year supported the conservatory's scholarship fund. The current lease gave the Asolo the option of continuing that support or paying its share of the building's utility bills. The Asolo board opted for the latter, because paying the bills would be less expensive. If this was the decision, Dean Wallace responded, the conservatory would leave at the end of the current term rather than in 2005. "If the Asolo isn't paying for scholarships, they would be just a tenant, and no longer a supporter of the conservatory."

A glimmer of hope shone on March 12, 2003. The spokesmen at FSU said that they would be willing to keep the conservatory in Sarasota if they could have more control and lose less money. Provost Abele added, "I don't think it can continue without a major reorganization of the [Asolo] board." A restructuring of the board, he pointed out, would allow the theatre to receive state matching funds for private donations, thereby cutting FSU's costs. Ron Greenbaum admitted that everything was negotiable. The provost said that before March 12, he felt sure the conservatory would stay in Sarasota, but he was "baffled" that the board was not willing to work out the details at that first meeting. Senator Carlton gave the board an April 9 deadline to respond.

Before the deadline, FSU proposed a list of particulars: first, the new board would be made up of four residents from Sarasota and Manatee Counties and three FSU officials. "Under the new proposal, local residents would be nominated by board members and appointed by the FSU president. The Asolo's [producing] artistic director…would report to the Florida State dean of theatre and could be fired by either the board of directors or the university president." Company members worried the Asolo would become a "suburb of Tallahassee."

Once again, and with the same shaky optimism, Howard Millman and Gil Lazier announced the mainstage and conservatory season for the coming year. The plays included *The Crucible*, *I'm not Rappaport* and *Arms and the Man*.

Meanwhile, the tennis match continued.

The two sides were attempting to work out a plan that would keep the conservatory in Sarasota. The Asolo proposed an arrangement similar to

By Ralph Smith of the Sarasota Herald-Tribune.

the one FSU had with the museum. "Under the DSO [Direct Support Organization]," read the proposal, "the Asolo would be run by a seven-member board of directors appointed by the FSU president: three members from FSU and four from the Sarasota-Manatee community. A larger advisory board would also have input. FSU will offer a counter-proposal."

Apparently not much progress was made during this first week in April 2003. Provost Abele suggested that a "fresh set of faces" might give the negotiations more perspective and positive energy. Esther Mertz was adamant that the partnership between the theatre and the university continue. Her trustee, retired attorney Michael Close, had been one of the most active negotiators.

There were key issues that had to be worked out. Florida State's priorities:

> *1. More flexibility to schedule* [its own] *events in the theatre.*
> *2. To cut its costs surrounding the 30-student conservatory.*
> *3. To renegotiate the current Asolo lease, in which the theatre had been paying FSU $1 a year in rent. The current lease was set to expire in 2042.*

The Asolo wanted:

> *1. To continue the theatre lease, especially the 40-year term.*
> *2. To maintain the authority to have performances almost every day from November through May and possibly to expand by one play a season.*
> *3. Most members of a new governing board to be from Sarasota and Manatee counties.*
> *4. To keep the conservatory in Sarasota.*

By the end of April, both sides reported that some progress had been made. It was said that the meetings had been "amicable" and that the representatives were becoming "optimistic" about their progress. Robert Bradley, an FSU representative, reported, "We made good progress. But the devil's in the details."

FSU's share of funding the conservatory was now the most challenging point, one that had to be resolved before other matters (like combined marketing for the university and the theatre) could be considered. In May, president Wetherell said that if FSU continued to fund the conservatory and the Asolo to the degree it had in the past, such funding would now put a strain on the university's budget. Senator Carlton, chairwoman of the Senate education committee, hoped to procure enough money from the legislature to enable FSU to continue paying the $400,000 for Asolo salaries.

Third-year conservatory students received their diplomas on May 4, 2003. Each was given the opportunity to speak, and they expressed great praise for their experiences at the Asolo—especially for the chance to play major roles with the resident company. First- and second-year students hoped they would have a chance to stay in Sarasota and eventually participate in the same ceremony. The professional actors, too, dreaded the prospect of losing the conservatory. Each of us in the professional company mentored at least one student, and the resulting personal relationships were treasured.

The university was now considering allowing the program to stay in Sarasota if students could spend the first two years in Tallahassee, or if they could receive more training in film and television.

Then came good news. Negotiators agreed on the framework of a deal that would keep the conservatory in Sarasota for the full three years. Senator Carlton said that guaranteeing a new class "would make it easier for her to justify placing an extra $1.1 million in the state budget. And instead of directly paying the salaries of six Asolo employees, FSU would enter into a contract with the Asolo for the specific services it expects."

Members of the Asolo board unanimously approved a tentative agreement with FSU. The ball was now in FSU's court as Sarasota waited to see if president Wetherell would sign the agreement. Mid-May was a late time to recruit a new class for the coming fall, but on May 22, legislative leaders agreed to a budget that included the essential $1.1 million. President Wetherell signed the agreement.

When the dust finally settled, the Asolo board kept its autonomy. FSU paid the Asolo $240,000 to train its students, and the Asolo paid $10,000 per student for their assistantships, including the trip to London.

After a benefit for the conservatory on Sunday, May 20, Esther Mertz's attorney, Michael Close, felt obligated to address some of the press coverage that had occurred during the fallout of the negotiations:

> *I write regarding the Charlie Husking column May 20 titled "Celebrating the FSU/Asolo Conservatory." It is terribly wrong to single out Dr. Larry Abele for ridicule as Husking did by saying there was "no truth to the rumor that there will be a dunking booth" for the FSU provost. Indeed, Dr. Abele is to be congratulated as the father of the solution of the problem, for he came up with the original idea of "fresh start" negotiations, using negotiators who were new to the process. Moreover, focusing on personalities is a threat to the new beginning that the four negotiators saw in the agreement that they reached May 16, an agreement which completely resolves the fracture in the partnership. We have the chance and the framework for a fresh start that benefits all concerned. Let's keep it that way.*

Michael Close's diplomatic skills were cited as a major factor in calming the acrimony between the two sides. He and Senator Carlton had become heroes to the community for directing the battle to keep the conservatory in Sarasota, though neither had known a great deal about the program when they began. Esther Mertz was responsible for Close's involvement; Senator Carlton had been invited by Ron Greenbaum, and she took the time to come to Sarasota and see firsthand what the Asolo and the conservatory meant to its region. "I quickly learned how deeply people felt about the conservatory, how much a part of the fabric of life of southwest Florida it was," she said. "And I went from knowing nothing about the program to becoming a true believer myself."

Provost Abele received credit for encouraging a new group of negotiators to address the issues. It was Close who mediated those talks between Asolo representatives Don Schoenbaum and Nancy Markle and FSU's Robert Bradley and Lyn Weick. "A fresh approach was necessary," said Close, because Greenbaum and Abele "are strong personalities, and they were talking past each other, or over each other."

"He has this uncanny ability to listen to different opinions and cut to the chase," said Carlton of Close, "to translate strong opinions into an agreement everyone can live with."

A short time after the settlement, there was a conservatory benefit at which the students and faculty cheered Michael Close, Lisa Carlton and Esther Mertz. The evening ended with everyone singing "You Gotta Have Heart."

Simultaneously, Sarasotans jeered Dean Steven Wallace. The provost, however, expressed full confidence in Wallace, arguing that the problems were the result of previous interim deans who'd had "a light hand on the tiller in those years." For his part, the dean contended that the criticism had come from only a handful of students. He expressed full confidence about the future, saying, "Together we will help each other as we continue the transition from the old system to the new guy."

Finally, in late May 2004, the Asolo and FSU signed an operating accord: the conservatory would remain in Sarasota at least until 2006. The community rejoiced.

But almost immediately, another absurd melodrama erupted. Gil Lazier had declared his intentions to retire from teaching at the end of the 2003–4 term. Dean Wallace had wanted a successor appointed by January 2004 "so that person can work with Gil, take advantage of his institutional memory"—but no successor was named. On Sunday evening, May 23, 2004, just two days before Lazier's scheduled retirement, a gala dinner (and roast) celebrated his career. Dean Wallace was among the guests.

The next morning at nine o'clock, Wallace, accompanied by security guards, entered Gil Lazier's office at the center and ordered him to clear out his desk and be out of the building by the end of the day.

Because of his tenure with FSU, Gil technically could not be fired; but Kate Holgate, the much-beloved coordinator of academic support services, could be—and was. The students described the forty-eight-year-old Holgate as a compassionate, indispensable figure who helped solve all of their problems, from conservatory issues to tax and health insurance concerns.

Conservatory faculty member Margaret Eginton, who was appointed interim director, urged the students to try and remain positive. "Despite the day's events," she said, "the program is in a position to thrive and succeed."

Once again, Charlie Husking provided his own narration of the ordeal:

> *Don't they teach public-relations classes at Florida State University? I'd guess not, judging from the way FSU tarnished its image, outraged local residents and alienated current and potential donors last week. What reason other than public embarrassment did Wallace have for ordering Lazier to pack his things and leave the FSU center the day before he was to retire? "This is a vindictive act by a petty bureaucrat, designed to humiliate two dedicated professionals* [Lazier and Holgate] *who have always acted in the students' best interest," said Sharon Spelman, an Asolo Theatre Company actress. That's strong stuff, but it reflects the sentiment in dozens of calls and e-mails I've received this week. At a time when FSU is trying to increase its presence in the community, the university is starting to have all the appeal of a toxic waste dump.*

Provost Abele assured all interested that the School of Theatre was not being eliminated or demoted in status; it was "simply getting new leadership and likely more focused instruction." Dean Wallace requested reassignment so he could work as a consultant on the restoration of the historic Asolo and other special projects.

It should be noted that this brief episode was a stark anomaly in the remarkable collaboration that had always existed between FSU and the Asolo. With the air cleared, all that was left was to restore the historic relationship that had done so much good for both the university and the theatre.

Chapter 18

Happily Ever After

I think if everyone is comfortable, they might be asleep by intermission.
—Michael Donald Edwards

With the new stability, there was less and less melodrama to impede the flow of progress.

Greg Leaming became the director of the FSU/Asolo Conservatory in the spring of 2005. (He also became the theatre's associate artistic director.) His credits included director of artistic programming for Long Wharf Theatre, artistic director of the Portland Stage Company and associate artistic director at Hartford Stage Company. "I wasn't a player in the events that happened before," he said, "and it's important that the community understand it's a new environment, that positive things are happening here." It was the kind of reassurance that the Asolo supporters needed to hear. Leaming wanted to raise the profile of the conservatory and give more attention to the plays the second-year students presented in the Cook Theatre. "This is a great program," he said, "and it has the potential to become even better and to play an even more vital role in the community."

Michael Donald Edwards directed *Smell of the Kill* for the Asolo in January 2005. The following May, after an extensive search, he was named the Asolo's new producing artistic director. He would have a year to work with Howard Millman before taking his place.

Edwards, a native of Australia, received his BA degree at Monash University in Australia and his MFA degree at UCLA. He'd been associate artistic director for Syracuse Stage and earlier served as artistic director

Michael Donald Edwards. *Photo by Gary W. Sweetman.*

for Shakespeare Santa Cruz in California. His résumé as director included work in theatres across this country and beyond: the Oregon Shakespeare Festival, the Old Globe in San Diego, Victoria Opera, the Metropolitan Opera in New York City, the Israeli Vocal Arts Institute in Tel Aviv, the Julliard School and many other theatres in the United States, England and Australia.

Howard Millman retired on June 30, 2006. (Though "retirement" may be a misnomer; he continues working in local theatres.) A placid dynamo, he was one of the few who would prove to be as adept at the artistic side of theatre as he was dealing with the nuts and bolts of financial matters. He was also a people person who understood the importance of maintaining a strong tie with the community, and on two occasions Howard was a major factor in keeping the Asolo alive. He was and is a dear friend. A gloriously appropriate gala celebrated his two tenures at the Asolo.

Edwards immediately began his tenure as producing artistic director. Edwards's first season at the Asolo included *Amadeus* (which he also directed), *Men of Tortuga*, *A Few Good Men* and *Darwin in Malibu*. "Do you want to produce comfortable theatre?" he asked. "I think if everyone is comfortable, they might be asleep by intermission. Art on some level must be challenging. When you can only receive information that reinforces what you already think, then you are saying that you don't want artists in your life. You don't want the questioners, the challengers." He would later write, "Theatre is necessary. It goes to the heart of what it is to live in a community. Paul Woodruff, in a wonderful new book, argues very persuasively that without the presence of theatre in some form we would never develop true empathy. And empathy is the fundamental building block of humaneness."

The theatre changed its name from Asolo Theatre Company to Asolo Repertory Theatre, in order to emphasize its repertory roots. A marketing campaign aimed to change the shorthand from "the Asolo" to "Asolo Rep."

Isa Thomas died in early April 2008. She had played some ninety-five roles at the Asolo, including Amanda in *The Glass Menagerie*, Penelope Sycamore in *You Can't Take It with You*, Serefina in *The Rose Tattoo*, Lady Macbeth, Juno in *Juno and the Paycock* and Mrs. Warren in *Mrs. Warren's Profession*. After leaving the Asolo, she moved to New York, where she enjoyed a successful career in film and television. She was a monumental talent and a loving friend.

Michael Edwards initiated a project in the fall of 2007 to build on the foundation of a sound relationship with the community and widespread respect that had been created and re-created over the years by the Asolo's visionaries.

Ron Sharpe and Barbara Russell were two producers looking for a theatre in which to showcase a musical intended for Broadway. These producers, both pragmatic businesspeople, decided that the Asolo had the right facilities and the right people to prepare this production for a New York showing. It turned out that they were right. *A Tale of Two Cities* played on the Mertz stage for five weeks, much of the time to packed houses that regularly gave standing ovations for the performances. (The complex set had been built by the Asolo Scenic Studio and would be transported to New York for the Broadway production.)

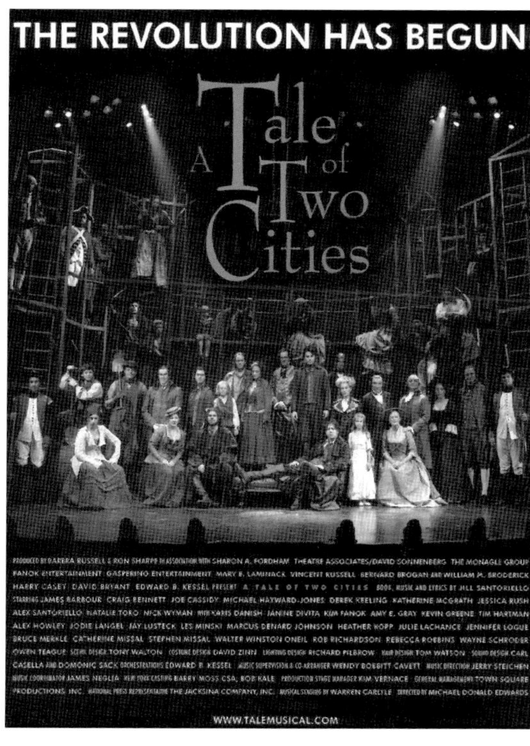

A Tale of Two Cities. Photo by Carol Rosegg.

"It certainly has raised the profile of the theatre and its attractiveness as a place to work," Edwards said. "It showed people

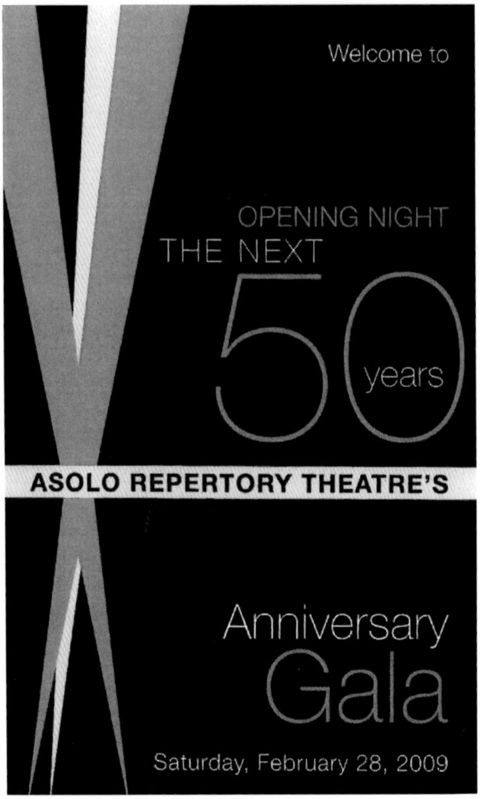

that we're able to create high-quality work and that it is a place for directors, designers and performers where they can do good work and they will be treated very well by the institution and everyone who has worked here."

A Tale of Two Cities was not well received by the critics in New York. Still, this in no way reflected on the Asolo, which demonstrated an ability to cope with the manifold demands of a sizeable Broadway production.

The musical *Barnum* opened the 2008–9 season—the Asolo's fiftieth. Although not a premiere, it was a spectacular success and would be followed by equally successful—and undeniably challenging—productions that included *Equus* and *A Winter's Tale*. "It puts us on the map as producing Broadway-quality work," Edwards said.

So the Asolo, as was true in the '60s and '70s, again received national praise for serving the hearts and minds of its region. It now garnered a reputation for showcasing major productions, and, at the same time, it maintained the rotating repertory and resident company, which existed as a visible and admired part of the community as a whole. These were the goals of Richard Fallon, Robert Strane, Eberle Thomas, Howard Millman and so many others, and they were once again pointing the Asolo in the right direction.

On the evening of February 28, 2009, a lavish black-tie gala celebrated the Asolo's fiftieth anniversary.

The Historic Asolo Theater was beautifully restored and placed in a new visitors' center near the FSU/Asolo Performing Arts Center. On the evening of October 6, 2006, a grand reopening celebrated the unique space that had inspired the first Asolo Festival almost fifty years before.

About the Author

Brad Wallace first came to the Asolo as a student actor in 1961, signed his first professional contract there in 1967 and, over the years, has appeared in over 160 Asolo productions. He also worked in other theatres across the country, including the Alabama, Colorado and Utah Shakespearian festivals, Pennsylvania Centre Stage, the Cape playhouse, the Barter Theatre, the Geva Theatre, American Stage and Florida Studio Theatre. He was the recipient of the Florida Professional Theatre Association's Richard G. Fallon Award in 1997. He and his stage manager wife, Marian, have been married for over forty-five years.